EASTERN VIEW OF JERUSALEM

*The Dome of the Rock and the
Gate Beautiful on Mount Moriah
can be seen from the eastern
hills of Jerusalem.*

Israel Revealed with Daniel Rona
P.O. Box 52
Sandy, Utah 84091 USA
e-mail: ensign@israelrona.com
Web Site: http://www.israelrevealed.com
(800) 272-RONA (7662)

ISBN: 0-9660231-6-1

*Charitable donations and proceeds from this book go
to The Ensign Foundation, which facilitates understanding
and exchanges between the peoples of Judah and Joseph. Your
contributions are gratefully accepted to The Ensign Foundation
(Internal Revenue Code 501c3 #87-0518).*

ISRAEL
REVEALED

**Discovering Mormon and Jewish Insights
in the Holy Land**

by
Daniel Rona

Photography by
Don O. Thorpe

The Olive Tree of Life

The eternal nature of life is mirrored in the evergreen *olive tree*.
Taking strength from its roots, it's branches give fruit.
Its perpetuity is lengthened by pruning and trimming.
Sometimes its branches are grafted into the nethermost part of the vineyard.
Other times, those branches are brought back to the mother tree to restore new life.

Noah discovered the restoration of life as the dove returned to the ark with *olive leaves*.
Later, the purest *olive oil* provided light in the Temple at Jerusalem.
Also, the Temple doors that represented entering into Eternal Life were made of *olive wood*.
And the beauty of Israel is described as the spreading branches and leaves of an *olive tree*.

Life's future gets its legacy from its past, an *olive tree* gets its life from its roots.
Ancient *olive wood* lasts long into the future, likewise life's past gives us direction in the future.
As an *olive tree* top is trimmed, new growth comes from the rods out of its roots.
The cycle of life and the *olive tree* are mirrored in "The first being last and the last being first."

Rabbis have said that the evergreen olive is a symbol that the people of Israel will ever live.
Israel's destiny preceded her. Her present is steadfast and her future is secured in the hands of God.
Yet, as olives are pounded and pressed to make oil, so must Israel be tempered.
In many ways, the *olive tree* could be the "Tree of Life"
and through Israel God gave the "Key of Life."

– Daniel Rona –

Dedicated to my father, Dr. Herbert (Rosenthal) Rona.
He followed the prompting of his heart.
It led him to the Land of Israel;
It led him to the Land of Zion;
It led him to the Lord.

Excerpts from Jacob 5, The Book of Mormon

3. For behold, thus saith the Lord, I will liken thee, O house of Israel, like unto a tame olive-tree, which a man took and nourished in his vineyard; and it grew, and waxed old, and began to decay.

14. And it came to pass that the Lord of the Vineyard went his way, and hid the natural branches of the tame olive-tree in the nethermost parts of the vineyard, some in one and some in another, according to his will and pleasure.

51. And the Lord said...

52. Wherefore, let us take of the branches of these which I have planted in the nethermost parts of my vineyard, and let us graft them into the tree from whence they came...

63. Graft in the branches; begin at the last that they may be first, and that the first may be last, and dig about the trees, both old and young, the first and the last; and let the last and the first, that all may be nourished once again for the last time

Jerusalem Wall and "Citadel" by the Jaffa Gate.

Acknowledgements

 Many people have given of themselves to bring this synopsis of Israel to you. My desires to publish glad tidings have been greatly inspired by my faithful and patient wife, Marilyn. Our five children also know how consumed our family is by the quest to reveal Israel to as many people as we can. I am very grateful for their insistence on teaching and sometimes correcting me in points of history and the Hebrew language. Our family is a wonderful combination of Joseph and Judah. We present this work to bring Judah and Joseph even closer together.

Another dedicated "Joseph" whom I thank from my heart is Dr. Daniel H. Ludlow, professor at Brigham Young University and a committed teacher and servant of the Lord. He is a friend and has been a powerful influence. I stand humbled by his generous counsel and kindness. I am grateful to John Tvednes, senior researcher at the Foundation for Ancient Research and Mormon Studies (FARMS), for teaching me, by example, how to learn. The continuous friendship of Don O. Thorpe, along with his photographic and creative artistry, has made possible the film series and book, *ISRAEL REVEALED*.

It is a pleasure to also recognize Marvin Goldstein, Lex de Azevedo, Kurt Bestor, Janice Kapp Perry, Michael McLean, Bryce Neubert and Merrill Jenson for the contributions they have made to the Israel Revealed tours through their music. Their music contributed much to the spirit of understanding the life of the Savior in his land. The continuing friendship of Dr. Stanley M. Wagner, Rabbi, blossomed with his participation in the tours. He has taught me much and has helped me focus on the ancient sources of Judaism.

Finally, I would like to thank all those who have supported our efforts and trusted me as their guide in the Holy Land.

— Daniel Rona

Part of the ancient wall around Old Jerusalem. The walls are a mixture of Herodian stones, that can weigh several tons, and Turkish rocks added many centuries later.

Foreword

This book is written in response to requests from many who have toured with me, asking that I put in print some of the stories and insights that explain how Jewish, Moslem and Christian traditions, doctrines, and cultures relate to each other and interact with Latter-day Saint beliefs. It is both a personal instructional witness of the land of my birth and a picture book which portrays the ancient wonders and modern beauty of Israel. It is my hope that the reader will be filled with feelings for the Savior, the prophets, and their land.

I write for those who have longed to go to the Holy Land but for one reason or another could not, and for those who have gone and want to relive the experience. I write for those who wish to see Israel from the perspective of a Jew who is a Latter-day Saint.

Many have wondered how I could be both a Jew and a Mormon. More than just religion is involved. Both become a culture and a lifestyle. Being born a Jew is a fact, much like being born American or Italian. When one becomes a Latter-day Saint in any region of the world, one is not asked to forget one's cultural roots. In fact, it is quite the opposite. Actually, understanding Jesus has deepened my gratitude for my Jewish roots.

I seek to share my heritage with you. I especially want my new "Family of Joseph" to better understand their own roots and ties with my "Family of Judah." Joseph Smith, Jr. was of the lineage of Joseph and Judah. I am one of the Tribe of Judah (a Jew) who has recognized the Messiah. My heritage is something I cherish. I can count myself with Jews who accepted "Jehoshua from Nazareth" as the awaited Messiah and their Savior.

"Understanding Jesus has deepened my gratitude for my Jewish roots. I seek to share my heritage with you."

The fact that Jesus was a Jew, and that he taught and acted "after the manner of the Jews" of his day, is worthy of consideration. He was and is the Jehovah of the Old Testament, the Lawgiver, and the promised Deliverer.

In 1974, as millions of Jews before me, I felt impressed to return to my homeland with my family. I also felt impressed to share my Jewish understanding of the Messiah with Latter-day Saints who desire to know about "the Galilean." It is for this reason that I became a licensed tour guide. If people cannot journey to the land itself, then I hope to bring a part of Israel to them through speaking engagements, videos, audio recordings and now this book.

My deepest love is for the Lord and his Gospel. What I know of Him causes me to love all mankind. He is the author of true and lasting peace. I sincerely seek to share the peace I have come to know and feel when walking in His footsteps in the Holy Land. Please hear my words as a whispered witness to the life and reality of Jesus of Nazareth.

Daniel shares LDS and Jewish insights with his tour companions

Daniel Rona
Jerusalem, 2001

About the Author

 Daniel Rona is the only licensed LDS guide in Israel. (Israeli law requires that every group touring in Israel have a licensed guide.) He has led more LDS Holy Land tours than all other tour operators combined. He has guided tours since 1974, and does so almost every week of the year. The fact that he is an American, an Israeli, a Mormon, and a Jew makes his perspective unique.

Daniel Rona, son of Herbert Rosenthal and Kate (Kitty) Ettlinger, was born Daniel Denis Rosenthal in 1941, in what was then called Palestine. His German-Jewish parents escaped the Holocaust; his paternal grandparents did not. Daniel went to New York City with his father, Dr. Herbert Rosenthal, when his parents divorced.

Daniel was raised observing traditional Jewish holidays. However, his father was troubled with the loss of both of his parents at Auschwitz, along with six million other Jews who died in the war. He did not understand how the Jews could have been allowed to perish without at least a warning from God. He began investigating different religions as he searched for answers to his questions. He was offended by several Christian churches who wanted him to convert and abandon his Jewish life. He found a completely different attitude and doctrine among the "Mormons," who refused to baptize him until he understood that by doing so it was fulfilling a step in his Jewish life.

"He is unique in that he is an American, an Israeli, a Christian, and a Jew."

Shortly after his father became a member of the LDS Church, he and Daniel moved to Salt Lake City, Utah. Daniel's father married a Mormon convert, Jacqueline Arbogast. Daniel's mother also married Zvi Tohar, who became Chief Pilot of El Al Airlines. Tohar was the pilot who flew Adolf Eichman out of Argentina and back to Israel for his Holocaust trial. The dramatic account of this mission is documented in the book and motion picture called, "The House on Girabaldi Street."

Though the younger Rosenthal grew up in Salt Lake City, he never lost his Jewish individuality. He was comfortable with his unique nature, being a Jew and a Mormon. He developed a strong sense of gratitude for the freedoms and opportunities associated with being an American. When Daniel and his father became naturalized citizens of the United States, their family name was officially changed to Rona, his father's pen-name, coinciding with a new start in their lives.

Daniel's LDS mission call came with irony and joy: this nice Jewish-Mormon boy was to teach the gospel in Germany. Since then, Daniel has continued to teach the gospel to the German people and throughout the world.

After a successful mission, Daniel asked Area President Theodore M. Burton for permission to visit his mother and stepfather in Israel before returning to Utah. President Burton told him it was not only permissible but it was his responsibility to go. On his return to Utah, Apostle Ezra Taft Benson asked Daniel to report his mission, and more importantly, his experiences in Israel. Daniel's visit to his homeland of Israel started fires burning within him that would cause his family to move to the Holy Land to live eleven years later.

Shortly after he returned to Utah, he met Marilyn Minardi (who also had accepted the gospel when living in Cheyenne Wyoming in 1956). They were married in the Salt Lake Temple. Their children, David and Susan were born in Salt Lake City; Steven was born in St. Louis, Missouri; Joshua and Deborah were born in Israel. All five children (including Susan and Deborah) served in the Israeli Army prior to going on their full-time missions for the LDS church.

Daniel had a successful career in broadcasting, working for KSL Radio in Salt Lake City, and stations in New York, Chicago, St. Louis and later for the Voice of Israel. The outbreak of the "Six Day War" in Israel (1967) had such an impact on him that he immediately considered going back to Israel. But the conflict ended in less than a week. This experience and his feelings about leaving the U.S. were unsettling. When the "Yom Kippur War" broke out in 1973, Daniel, then in St. Louis, carefully avoided contact with any news media because he didn't want to deal with the forces that were "pulling him back to Israel." The pull came anyway. He felt he had to return to his navtive land.

Marilyn offered her husband her full support. Daniel suggested a familiarization trip to Israel, which they made in December 1973. By August 1974, they had sold their home and most of their belongings, survived two major financial setbacks, packed fifteen bags and suitcases, shipped a small car, a few beds, dishes and personal effects, and arrived in Israel with only $200, but no debt.

New immigrants to Israel usually get some kind of absorption and financial aid, but someone had notified the immigration authorities that Daniel and his family were "not Jews," but that they were "Mormons" coming to "broadcast" for the Mormon Church. Hence, he was denied the right to citizenship, despite the fact that Daniel had been born in that very land. Among other things, the denial meant they did not have permission to be employed. Since Daniel had been impressed to pack some carpentry tools, paint brushes and rollers in his suitcases, he began to solicit odd jobs, repairs and painting. Thereby, his family was able to eat, and they paid their own way without any government assistance. Eventually, the Ronas received Israeli citizenship.

The house painting business grew. At the same time, numbers of Latter-day Saints had been traveling to the Holy Land, hoping that they would experience the spirit of the land and the people. Unfortunately, they were often disappointed. It is a law in Israel that all tour groups must have a licensed Israeli guide. Israeli guides were generally not religious and had limited Mormon insights.

Daniel Rona sharing Jewish insights of the Beatitudes while overlooking the Sea of Galilee.

Being a local resident and ethnically rooted in Israel, Daniel saw the need to provide a professional, as well as a spiritually fulfilling touring experience. Making a career change, he was accepted, after two years of training in the Ministry of Tourism Course for Guides at the Hebrew University campus. He qualified as a licensed guide with the highest possible score on his final exam. Later, Daniel became a licensed transportation/and incoming tour operator through another extensive Ministry of Tourism course. Daniel Rona today is the only LDS licensed guide and tour operator in Israel.

Daniel has served as the Jerusalem Branch President, a member of the District Presidency, and District High Council, as a teacher, a counselor, and as President of the Jerusalem BYU Student Branch. Daniel is the founder of the nonprofit, charitable, Ensign Foundation, which creates bridges of understanding and exchanges of science and technologies as well as cultural and religious activities between Latter-day Saints and Israel. Specifically, he is interested in helping establish the House of Israel (both the peoples of Joseph and Judah) as an ensign to the world.

These Arab boys pace back and forth under the arches of the Dome of the Rock mosque as they memorize the Koran - the scriptures of Islam.

Don O. Thorpe

Photographer

Don Thorpe has traveled throughout the world photographing, writing, interviewing, and researching people and places for Christian organizations and publications. He has many years experience in media communications and production as an audio/visual producer and director, script writer, and photographer. He is an accomplished photo journalist, teacher, and lecturer.

Don is the author of the book *Available Light Photography*, published by Watson-Guptill of New York. His photographs have also appeared in major photographic publications and won numerous awards. His experience with many cultures and peoples gives his photographs human appeal and insight.

The photographic works published in the book *"Israel Revealed"* were selected from the tens of thousands of photographs Don has taken of Israel. Many of them are featured in the *"Israel Revealed"* video tapes.

"His experience with many cultures and peoples gives his photographs human appeal and insight."

Don Thorpe with children on the old triumphal-entry road to the temple in Jerusalem.

Contents

Scriptures reading on location.

Jewish family outing.

Latter-day shepherdess.

Beatitudes today.

Pilgrims' anticipation.

Coming of age Bar Mitzvah.

A Holy Sepulcher Priest.

Moslems approaching worship.

*Gate Beautiful, awaiting
the Savior.*

Marriage at Temple Wall.

Photographs

Solitary road to Bethlehem.

Entering His empty tomb.

Arab with modern camel.

Israeli billboard.

"Have you heard..."

- Overview -
The way of the sea

An **INTRODUCTION** to the land reveals that it is the **CROSSROADS OF THE EAST**. Modern **TEL AVIV**, ancient **JAFFA**, and the surrounding towns make up the largest Jewish city in the world, with over a million people in this area. Tel Aviv was established in 1910 on sand dunes. Continuing along the beautiful Mediterranean Coast, you reach **CAESAREA**, where ruins of Turkish, Crusader and Roman civilizations are visible. The Apostle Paul spent time imprisoned here. The restored theater is a dramatic place to review Paul's "almost" convincing speech to King Agrippa. A stop at **HAIFA**, Israel's third-largest city, gives you a breathtaking panoramic view of the largest harbor in Israel. Driving into the **JEZREEL VALLEY**, you can imagine the chariots of battle that were used on this battleground for six thousand years. Will **ARMAGEDDON** be next? The north side of the valley is **NAZARETH**, the boyhood home of Jesus. Nearby is **CANA**, where water was changed to wine. A short distance eastward is the **SEA OF GALILEE**; then our journey of discovery takes us northward to **KIBBUTZ KFAR GILADI**. This is an agricultural, collective settlement with additional industries, including a well-known guest inn.

The ruins of ancient Caesarea are scattered along this Mediterranean Sea Coast. Built by Herod the Great from 22 to 10 B.C., it was a majestic city with a theater, hippodrome, and luxuriant palaces. It even had a sewage system underneath the city.

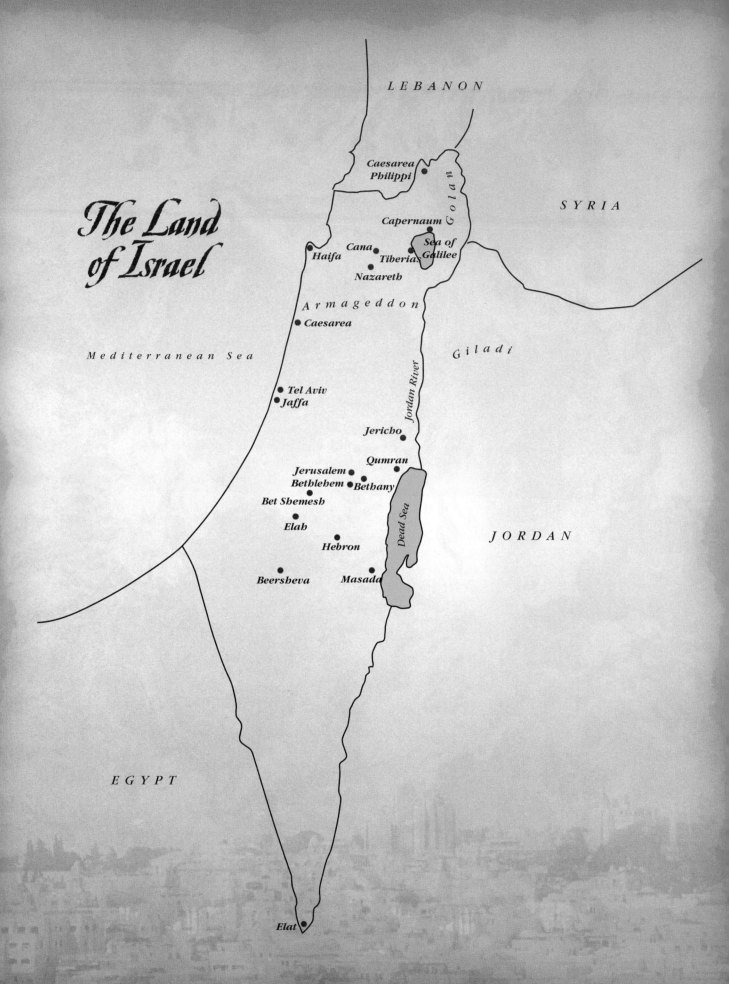

The Land of Israel

LEBANON

SYRIA

Caesarea Philippi

Golan

Capernaum

Cana
Haifa
Tiberias
Sea of Galilee
Nazareth

Armageddon

Caesarea

Giladi

Mediterranean Sea

Jordan River

Tel Aviv
Jaffa

Jericho

Qumran

Jerusalem
Bethlehem
Bethany
Bet Shemesh

Dead Sea

Elah

JORDAN

Hebron

Beersheva
Masada

EGYPT

Elat

Chapter 1

An introduction to the land

Land of Visible Contrasts

 The Age of Israel: Israel is a land of visible contrasts; it's a young nation built on an ancient inheritance. It is seven years younger than I am. I was born in Israel in 1941, and Israel only became a State in 1948. You see, on one hand Israel is just over fifty years old, and on the other hand, its history stretches back almost fifty centuries. Throughout this history, the land of Israel has been the focus of attention by its surrounding neighbors who inhabit vast areas of the Middle East.

Borders: The land of Israel is really quite small. The Bible borders are from the "Jordan River to the Mediterranean" and "Dan to Beersheva." Nowadays, the border is about sixty-five miles wide and about two hundred miles long.

Natural Resources: In this small area there are virtually no natural resources (no gold, silver, or metal deposits). Even Golda Meir, former Prime Minister of Israel and pleased to consider herself a secular Jewess, humorously chided Moses. She said, "He traveled the wilderness for forty years and then settled the one spot that had no oil!"

Conquests of Israel: From a perspective of treasure or riches there is no apparent reason for the almost thirty different conquests this land has experienced. The land of Israel gained the distinction of being the access to the two great regional centers of government. That justified the constant conquests.

Conquerors of Israel: The foreign masters attempting conquest included (chronologically): Canaanites, Egyptians, Hyksos, Midianites, Hittites, Philistines, Assyrians, Babylonians, Persians, Greeks, Syrians, Romans, Byzantines, Moslems, Mamelukes, Crusaders, Turks, and British. Yet none of them remained. Throughout its colorful history, the land of Israel was overrun, conquered, or inhabited close to thirty different times by at least nineteen different peoples.

Another distinction: The very Jews and Arabs who have experienced the various conquests are still here. They have survived, submitted to, or eventually overthrown foreign occupants. Foreign powers have not always been adverse; in fact, several of

"Israel is a land of visible contrasts; it's a young nation built on an ancient inheritance."

A group of orthodox Jews walk to their prayers at the Western Wall. Orthodox Jews usually dress in black clothes as a result of centuries-old customs that do not permit one to differentiate between "rich or poor."

them brought added prosperity and positive world influence to the local inhabitants. For example, the Roman era from 64 B.C. to about A.D. 100 was conducive to growth and education.

Conflicts Incorrectly Perceived: The Jews and Arabs view this land as their home. Yet, no legitimate Jewish or Arab government has called it mutually exclusive. For the most part, they have successfully coexisted for centuries. The struggles in the twentieth century were more between Arabs and Arabs than the perceived Arab/Jewish conflicts.

Reasons for Conquest: The reasons for the foreign conquests were not economic in the sense of resources to plunder; they were geographic. Israel is situated between two great population centers. To the north and east is the Fertile Crescent with its millions of people; to the south and west is the fertile Nile Delta with its millions of people. These major Middle-East population centers wanted to correspond and trade with each other. They traveled through the land of Israel, and it became the Crossroads of the East.

Crossroads of the East: To make a point, let me relate a story. A few years ago I was invited (among others) to audition for the Spoken Word broadcasts of the Mormon Tabernacle Choir. I suggested that since Jerusalem was my home, I would always be ready to be their resident announcer in Israel. For more than seven decades, the program began with the words, "From the Crossroads of the West." However, I would probably begin the broadcasts with the words, "From the Crossroads of the East." This little word game, a chiasmus actually, contains a clue to understanding the position of Latter-day Saints in America and their relationship with their brothers and sisters in Israel.

A Chiasmus of History

Meaning of a Chiasmus: Chiasmi are word games with subtle meanings. They are words listed in inverted repetitions or in opposites. For example: In ancient days (1), in the Crossroads of the East (2), there were living prophets (3). People had to come in (4), to the land of Israel from every direction to get the word. On the other hand, (4) the word of God is, (3) being sent out from, (2) living prophets headquartered in, (1) the Crossroads of the West. When you look in the middle, you see the One, who, in the meridian of times, was called by the Apostle John, "the Word." He is the source of truth, the center of focus. This word play, based on inversion or repetition of opposites, is a chiasmus. It is typical of many scriptural dialogues, reports of biblical events, and the way many historical events unfolded. It may be a way of considering the past as a guideline to the future.

A chiasmus can be words or thoughts listed first in one direction,

        1 -

            2 -

                3 -

                    4 etc.,

and then repeated in reverse order,

                    4 -

                3 -

            2 -

        1 -

The Chiasmus Center: A chiasmus is most valuable when the center point or apex is recognized. It is in the middle of the "crossroads chiasmus" that we find the source of truth, the Word, the Messiah, the Jehovah of the Old Testament, the Jesus of the New Testament, the Anointed One. God chose the land of Israel in which to reveal the truth, to send the Word in the ancient and meridian times.

> *In the beginning was the Word, and the Word was with God, and the Word was God.   JOHN 1:1*

> *Therefore, in the beginning the Word was, for he was the Word, even the messenger of salvation—*

> *The light and the Redeemer of the world; the Spirit of truth, who came into the world, because the world was made by him, and in him was the life of men and the light of men.*
> *DOCTRINE & COVENANTS 93:8-9*

In modern times he again sent the Word, revealed the truth, restored the spirit of discernment, and chose the free land of America to restore the truths for all the world. The word is going out through an impressive missionary effort to the world, instead of the world coming to the word.

Imagery of Israel

Green and Peaceful: Beyond the imagery of words, we find the land of Israel also contains majestic imagery of landscapes as varied as her people. It is a land with ocean, seas, plains, and mountains. It is green, and there is water. It is a good land, where Jews, Moslems, and Christians raise their families. Most of them agree that a feeling of peace and youthful growth exists here, as it has through the ages. Its history is almost as old as civilization itself. The distinction is unique: a new country growing into adulthood and yet consumed with its history.

So called "Lilies of the Field," these
beautiful red flowers are actually
Anenomes, which look like poppies.
They are a very hardy flower that grows
almost everywhere in Israel. They were
often used as symbols of beauty in the
Savior's parables and teachings.

Buildings in the Old City of Jerusalem are a blend of many cultures and styles. The walled-in city has four basic quarters: Jewish, Christian, Armenian and Moslem. Many holy sites are divided with portions for different ethnic religious groups.

Traveling in Israel: As mentioned, Israel is a land of travelers. Even today, over two million visitors a year come from all over the world to see, hear, and touch history and religion as it might have been in the past. Looking at Israel's borders as they were anciently reveals the same lesson. The routes from the northern Fertile Crescent to the southern fertile Egyptian Nile Delta truly became the Crossroads of the East.

> *And there shall be an highway for the remnant of his people,*
> *which shall be left, from Assyria; like as it was to Israel in the day*
> *that he came up out of the land of Egypt.   ISAIAH 11:16*

Come! Journey with me through the land that has touched the hearts of hundreds of millions of travelers. Meet the people, experience their customs, traditions, and religion. This ancient inheritance revealed to prophets includes simple truths that have evolved into many complex interpretations.

Holy Sites or Tourist Traps: In the land of Israel, religious traditions compete fiercely for attention, creating a wilderness of confusion. Over the years, "nonsites" have become "holy sites." Many of them have become monuments or, more precisely, tourist traps. However, if you look, listen, and feel, you'll be seeing the path, hearing the voice, and finding that "spiritual oasis in the Holy Land!"

Finding the Truth

Four Considerations: The triumph of learning is in recognizing the truth. Israeli guides joke that the more often they repeat a story, the truer it becomes! However, something as important as the Holy Land, with its history, religion, and culture, offers four simple considerations to be your guidelines to help determine the truth:

1. Archaeology: This is a systematic excavating research that reveals levels of civilizations. It is fortunate that almost every one of the conquerors had such a desire for personal ownership that they destroyed, covered, and rebuilt the cities they vanquished. Today we have discovered ancient cities that had up to 28 levels of civilization. Biblical cities such as Jerusalem, Jericho, Hebron, Gezer, Megiddo, and Hazor are some major examples of multilevel ruins. The scriptures allude to this science of discovery:

> *...Awake and sing, ye that dwell in dust: for... the earth shall cast*
> *out the dead.*

> *...the earth also shall disclose her blood, and shall no more cover*
> *her slain.   ISAIAH 26:19, 21*

> *...for the earth shall be full of the knowledge of the Lord as the*
> *waters cover the sea.*

> *Wherefore, the things of all nations shall be made known; yea, all*
> *things shall be made known unto the children of men.*

> *There is nothing which is secret save it shall be revealed; there is*
> *no work of darkness save it shall be made manifest in the light;*
> *and there is nothing which is sealed upon the earth save it shall*
> *be loosed.*   2 NEPHI 30:15-17

2. *Written Historical Accounts:* There are ever-increasing discoveries of recorded events. (Some of these ancient reports rival today's best-sellers.) These are the events that shaped the cultures and religions of the Middle East. In addition to the holy scriptures, many periods of civilization produced other written records. Dispatches and other letters on stone, clay, and metal tablets reveal important historical, governmental, and religious details and messages. Would you believe that names were changed to protect the innocent (and guilty)? Now, we've discovered who they really were. Many of these accounts directly coincide with biblical accounts. Written records have been and still are very important. You will discover:

> *...that the books were opened;...the dead were judged out of those*
> *things which were written in the books, according to their works;*
> *consequently, the books spoken of must be the books which*
> *contained the record of their works, and refer to the records which*
> *are kept on the earth. And the book which was the book of life is*
> *the record which is kept in heaven; the principle agreeing precisely*
> *with the doctrine which is commanded you in the revelation*
> *contained in the letter which I wrote to you previous to my*
> *leaving my place—that in all your recordings it may be recorded*
> *in heaven.*   DOCTRINE & COVENANTS 128:7

3. *Tradition:* Remember "Fiddler on the Roof" and "Tradition"? Every guide seems to get away with murder (of history) by saying, "Tradition says, ..." The term is often used, but it is the least reliable when referring to the buildings and "holy sites" spanning Israel. Ah! But the most credible traditions are those of the names and places. You see, most of the names of cities and towns are still the same or of close linguistic connection to their ancient names. For example, Salem is now Jeru<u>salem</u>. Bethlehem is still Bethlehem. Nazareth is still Nazareth, and many more. Here is an example from the Bible:

> *And he called it Shebah: therefore the name of the city is Beersheba*
> *unto this day.*   GENESIS 26:33

4. *Feelings:* (Now this gets very personal.) You can feel the significance of places and events through the spirit that touches your heart. People yearn for this influence when they ponder religion. People have spiritual feelings based on their own religious expectations. However, Israel generates feelings of peace—a sense of hallowedness and awe that time has not erased. I know that you will feel an increased sense of understanding by reading the scriptures where they occurred. There's nothing like it in the whole world. Here is a wonderful key to understanding true feelings:

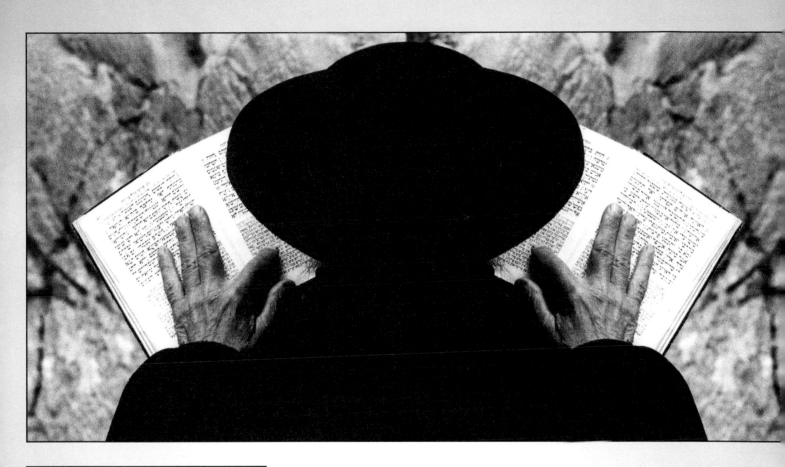

The scriptures have special meaning for the Jews. Many orthodox Jews in Jerusalem make it a daily practice to read from the Torah at the Western Wall.

Now, we will compare the word unto a seed. Now, if ye give place, that a seed may be planted in your heart, behold, if it be a true seed, or a good seed, if ye do not cast it out by your unbelief, that ye will resist the Spirit of the Lord, behold, it will begin to swell within your breasts; and when you feel these swelling motions, ye will begin to say within yourselves—It must needs be that this is a good seed, or that the word is good, for it beginneth to enlarge my soul; yea, it beginneth to enlighten my understanding, yea, it begin-neth to be delicious to me.   ALMA 32:28

With these principles as guidelines, the chance of your understanding truth rather than presuming fiction increases dramatically. The heartfelt joy of the Holy Land can be experienced by remembering the events that took place here. On one hand, great events were caused by humble prophets; and on the other, men wanting to be great were caused to be humble. The contrasts intensify and expand our vision. In Israel nowadays, there's a saying, "How odd of God to choose the Jews." For God's own reasons, He chose this land and its inhabitants to be the place and the people for revelation of truth.

Let's go back before there were "Jews." You'll remember that Abraham, apparently the first Hebrew, lived in the East in the land of the Chaldees. Later we'll discuss more about how he was sent west to the fertile Mediterranean coastal region to establish the true worship of God. In any case, religion and culture developed that eventually spread to the surrounding lands and peoples, and thus Israel became the spiritual and temporal Crossroads of the East. It is truly remarkable that such a little land had such a great effect on history.

A pause between prayers. Two Orthodox Jews seated by the Western Wall.

Chapter 2

The Way of The Sea

Jaffa

Ancient Seaport: Jaffa (Joppa) is an ancient Old Testament seafaring stop. In archaeological terms, it is a tel, a mound of different civilizations layered one on each other after each subsequent destruction and rebuilding. This particular way station also became a seaport, possibly the oldest seaport in history. Jaffa is where the ancient prophet Jonah left for the west instead of going east to Nineveh as the Lord commanded him to do.

Jonah: As the Bible relates, a terrible storm arose, endangering the ship and crew. Jonah, being identified as the cause, was thrown overboard, but the Lord did not let him perish. Instead Jonah spent three days and three nights inside the belly of a great fish.

> *Now the Lord had prepared a great fish to swallow up Jonah. And Jonah was in the belly of the fish three days and three nights. JONAH 1:17 (see also chapters 1 & 2)*

Jonah did not know that we, almost thirty centuries later, would be referring to his experience as a sign of the Messiah.

The entire account is so symbolic that it deserves a closer look. Instead of going north and east as the Lord instructed, Jonah went south and west. Instead of going up to Nineveh, he went down into the sea. All this seems to be a short-term defiance on Jonah's part, but the Lord Jehovah had a long-term lesson in mind. Jonah went down, personally, physically, and then the Lord brought him up. Jonah was dead (three days and three nights) and lived again. I suppose his account is one of the earliest "near death" accounts so popular today.

The popular expression about Jonah's experience is that "it's a whale of a story." Hold on! According to Jacques Cousteau, whales are rarely found in the Mediterranean. However, there exists a grouper fish that, according to experts, can grow large enough to swallow a man. There are modern tales that reveal such occurrences as well.

God's True Name: In reading Jonah's account, it becomes obvious that he learned a great lesson. His four chapters are an interesting study in contrasts and opposites. His is a testimony that has one purpose: to witness that the Lord saves. He says that clearly in chapter 2, verse 9, "Salvation is of the Lord." Since the word Jehovah is

"The center point is the Savior: "Salvation is for all people."

Jaffa, sometimes called Joppa, is an ancient seaport near the modern city of Tel Aviv. Jaffa was the main seaport in Israel at the time of Solomon. It is also famous because Jonah sailed from Jaffa before his experience inside a great fish.

unspeakable in Hebrew (it means I AM—and "I am" isn't even conjugated in Hebrew), a shortened version of Jehovah is found in "Jeho," "Jah" or "Jahweh." Names such as "Elijah" (my God is Jehovah), "Jeremiah" and "Hezekiah" all refer to "Yah." The word salvation is rendered with the shortened sound "sha" or "shua," such as in "Elisha" (my God saves). However, best of all is the Lord's name "Jeho-shua." This became "Joshua" and eventually that became "Jesus" in English. It means, "Jehovah saves," or as Jonah put it, "Salvation is of the Lord."

Messianic Sign of Jonah

The Pharisees asked Jesus for a sign that he was the Messiah—the Jehovah who saves. He informed them that a wicked and adulterous nation seeks for signs. Jesus reminded the Pharisees that they already had the one and only sign of the Messiah they would get.

Three Days and Three Nights: Jonah was in the sea for three days and three nights and then came alive again. Jesus prophesied that He would be three days and three nights in the earth and then live again in the resurrection.

> *But he answered and said unto them, An evil and adulterous generation seeketh after a sign; and there shall no sign be given to it, but the sign of the prophet Jonas:*
>
> *For as Jonas was three days and three nights in the whale's belly; so shall the Son of man be three days and three nights in the heart of the earth.   MATTHEW 12:39-40*

As those people listened, they may have heard his words, but many didn't see the real picture. At first, Jonah may not have seen the entire picture either.

Teach the Gentiles

Peter's Vision of the Sheet (Talith): In New Testament times, the city of Jaffa was some twenty feet below today's city level. Simon Peter was staying here at the home of Simon the Tanner when he received a remarkable vision. It was the sixth hour of the day (the sixth hour is what in modern times we call noon). Simon Peter apparently was praying (religious Jews pray three times a day, covering their heads and using a special prayer cloth, a *talith*, over their shoulders). During his prayers Peter saw a sheet with knitted or knotted corners—maybe like the typical Jewish prayer shawl, a *talith* with its knotted corners—filled with all sorts of common or unclean foods. Today, this would be called *unkosher*. An angel commanded Peter to eat of those foods, contrary to Jewish dietary law. The vision was a conflict (or contrast) in symbolism; the talith used in the Temple as a holy garment, its 613 knots and strings symbolizing the laws given by Moses, was now filled with foods forbidden by the Law of Moses. I hasten to point out that visions really do contain pictures and sounds that convey information.

Vision of Cornelius: Now, connecting Peter's vision with another experience creates an even clearer picture. On the previous day some thirty-five miles to the north at Caesarea, a Roman centurion named Cornelius received a vision at the "ninth hour" of the day. (Again, in modern times that is three o'clock in the afternoon.) In the vision, an angel told Cornelius to send for Peter so that he could teach Cornelius the truth. Incidentally, the time to travel the distance of thirty-five miles would take the better part of two days, or at least an overnight journey.

Unkosher: Cornelius' invitation to Peter arrived just as Peter was contemplating the meaning of the unusual vision of "unkosher" foods he had just been commanded to eat. He lodged his Roman guests overnight, then departed with them to Caesarea —which took a total of three nights and three days. Peter was soon to learn of the correlation of these two heavenly manifestations. When Peter arrived to visit in the house of the Roman Cornelius, again contrary to Jewish law and custom, he related that God had updated or changed the food laws of Israel.

> *Then Peter opened his mouth, and said, Of a truth I perceive that God is no respecter of persons:*
>
> *But in every nation he that feareth him, and worketh righteousness, is accepted with him.*   ACTS 10:34-35

Not just Israelites, but all peoples were able to become children of the covenant. The three nights and three days serves as a metaphorical reminder of Jehovah saving Jonah at Jaffa; and later from Jaffa came the distinctive reminder that He saves all!

Peter and Cornelius in a Chiasmus: The scriptural report of Peter and Cornelius is written in a chiasmus. First we read of Cornelius' vision; next we learn of Peter's vision. But when Peter arrives in Caesarea, the vision of Cornelius is repeated. The center point is about the Savior and that salvation is for all people.

> *Behold, God is my salvation; I will trust, and not be afraid: for the Lord JEHOVAH is my strength and my song; he also is become my salvation.*   ISAIAH 12:2

Tel Aviv

Nineteen hundred years later, a new city sprang up on sand dunes near Jaffa. Tel Aviv became Israel's largest population center, an international city of people from all over the world. The sand dunes, which incidentally had blown and washed up from Egypt, were subdued. This coastal range, the ancient plains of Sharon, was transformed from windswept, dusty dunes and pockets of rotting swamps to fertile green fields once again.

Tel Aviv, once considered Israel's largest city, now has a few thousand less in population than Jerusalem. By the mid 1990s, its internationalism included Israel's first McDonald's. That was, however, preceded by Israel's own *McDavid's*! A Hard Rock Cafe and various pizza chains have invaded Israel's "Miami Beach." The coastal marinas, hotels, and Jewish population make it close kin to the Florida coastal resorts.

Tel Aviv was founded in 1910. It is the hub of a 19 city cluster which is the largest metropolitan area of Israel.

*Caesarea was an important seaport and the
capital of Roman government in Palestine.
The harbor had a remarkable breakwater
built from concrete poured under water.
These arches demonstrate the Herodian
architectural skill of the period.*

Caesarea

Ancient Palestine Capital: About two millennia ago, starting about 22 B.C.E. (a scholastic adjustment referring to "before common era"—that is, before the time of Jesus), the egomaniac King Herod built a city on the windy sand dunes that line the Way of the Sea. He named it after his ruler, Caesar. About thirteen miles south of Mount Carmel, Caesarea became the capital of what Romans called Palestine. (The name in Hebrew and Arabic is *Phillistia*. The Romans may have renamed it so, to "spite" the Jews.) Caesarea was a remarkable city with a breakwater harbor that could be used all year round. The breakwater was constructed by creating wooden forms lowered into the water with stone weights and then filled with concrete poured into the forms under water.

Roman City in Judea: A splendid theater, amphitheater, sports hippodrome, and worship areas added to the modern, opulent Roman city in the province of Judea. To provide fresh water for a city that may have grown to sixty thousand in population, fresh running water was channeled from Mount Carmel about thirteen miles away. Remainders of the Roman aqueduct and other structures are still visible today.

King Agrippa Was Almost a Believer: At Caesarea a later Herod, Agrippa the Second, questioned the Apostle Paul about his Roman arrest. That arrest interrupted the planned Jewish execution of Paul in Jerusalem. Under Roman law, Jewish priests were not allowed to execute anyone, except for those involved with temple violations. Paul had apparently preached in the temple after his remarkable conversion, but he escaped stoning at the hands of Jewish priests because he was also a Roman citizen. The restored theater at Caesarea is a fitting place to review Paul's speech to the king. In telling his unusual conversion story, which included his direct vision of the resurrected Jesus, he challenged the king himself to believe. King Agrippa retorted,

> *...Almost thou persuadest me ... .*
>
> *And Paul said, I would to God, that not only thou, but also all that hear me this day, were both almost, and altogether such as I am, except these bonds.   ACTS 26:28-29*

"Almost" may count in the game of pitching horseshoes. However, a commitment to true belief must be wholehearted; "almost" is not enough!

Caesarea Destroyed: Caesarea became the place of Jewish revolt under Rabbi Akiva as early as the year 63 C.E. (Common Era—again, a scholastic adjustment that means the same as A.D.). It later became a seat of Jewish learning and also Christian schools, including institutions founded by Origen and Eusebius. Eventually the city was destroyed by Moslems in the seventh century. Later, Crusaders rebuilt Caesarea as a much smaller place, surrounded it with a moat, and used the ruins of Herod's breakwater as a seaport.

The excavations at Caesarea are ongoing. The city is being rebuilt and some ancient facilities are being restored for modern use. In archaeological discoveries, a great amount of glass has been found. Some of it dates back at least two thousand years.

The Romans had a technique of mixing silver in the molten glass. This resulted in an iridescent glow to the glass. Now, twenty centuries later, the broken pieces of glass are used in unique jewelry pieces. There's a metaphor in this. Our lives can be average, and like ancient glass without silver, fairly dull. However, with pure religion, keeping ourselves unspotted from the vices of the world, we can actually sparkle.

> *Pure religion and undefiled before God and the Father is this, To visit the fatherless and widows in their affliction, and to keep himself unspotted from the world.*   JAMES 1:27

Haifa

Israel's Third-Largest City: Continuing further north on the coastal Way of the Sea, we find the city of Haifa rising splendidly upon Mount Carmel. The harbor was built by the British in the 1930's. They put in a breakwater to accommodate the larger ships and tankers of modern times. The area, which anciently was the inheritance of the tribe of Zebulun, is now the industrial center of Israel.

> *And the third lot came up for the children of Zebulun according to their families: and the border of their inheritance was unto Sarid:*
>
> *And their border went up toward the sea..*   JOSHUA 19:10-11

Thriving Industries: Oil refineries, steel mills, and manufacturing industries thrive in this city where one of the finest technical universities of the Western world is found. Haifa's "Technion" or Institute of Technology is the center for "high tech" in the Middle East. Haifa is known for its advances and accomplishments in technical and computer sciences. It is referred to as "silicone wadi." Haifa is the third-largest city in Israel with over a third of a million inhabitants. Due to the industry and cultural flair of the city, it has become known as the city with a higher standard of living. There's a saying relating to the three main Israeli cities, "You come to Haifa to pay, Tel Aviv to play, but to Jerusalem to pray."

Baha'i World Center: In Haifa, the Baha'i religion has its world center. The Baha'i have close to 5 million members throughout the world. Sorely persecuted in Persia (Iran) in the mid 1800's, they established new headquarters on Mount Carmel. Among the beliefs of this religion is the doctrine that all men are brothers and that they should speak the same language. The Baha'i teach their special language in worship centers. They also believe that their religion will rule and judge all people at the last days, before the "end of the world." Recently they have built a new justice center near their gold-domed headquarters building in Haifa on Mount Carmel.

Mount Carmel

Elijah and the Priests of Baal: Mount Carmel is most famous for the contest between Elijah and the priests of Baal, which was precipitated by the three-and-a-half years of drought. During the forty-two months of drought, Elijah was not able

THE SEAPORT CITY OF HAIFA

Haifa is Israel's third largest city, and the largest seaport in Israel. The city is built on the slopes of Mt. Carmel, and is compared to San Francisco and Hong Kong because of its view. Haifa is also the world center for the Baha'i faith.

to convince the Israelites that they should humble themselves and believe in Jehovah, the God of Israel. Elijah (his name means "My God is Jehovah") had an experience that would be used by Jesus nine centuries later as a powerful metaphor. Although there were many widows in Israel during his time, Elijah chose to bless a widow in Sarepta, a city by Sidon (Lebanon). She agreed to feed Elijah, even though her scant supply of flour and oil would be depleted. A miracle occurred after feeding the prophet. The widow's flour and oil supply continued through the remainder of the drought.

> *And she went and did according to the saying of Elijah: and she, and he, and her house, did eat many days.*

> *And the barrel of meal wasted not, neither did the cruse of oil fail, according to the word of the Lord, which he spake by Elijah.*
> *1 KINGS 17:15-16*

Fire from Heaven: Suffering from the lack of rain, King Ahab called for a contest in which he commanded Elijah and the 450 priests of Baal to prove which of their gods was the real god. The priests, skilled in dramatizations and theatrics, tried to call down fire from their gods of wind, fire, and rain to burn their offering. In spite of their attempts, nothing happened. Elijah let them fail again and again. He even taunted and teased them somewhat. This show was going to be the Lord's, not the priests'.

> *It came to pass at noon, that Elijah mocked them, and said, Cry aloud: for he is a god; either he is talking, or he is pursuing, or he is in a journey, or peradventure he sleepeth, and must be awaked.*
> *1 KINGS 18:27 (see also 17-46)*

Elijah then built another altar, dug a trench around it, and poured water on his offering, filling the trench. He then commanded fire from heaven to consume the offering. Not only was the offering consumed, but the water as well. The priests of Baal suffered a humiliating defeat and were later put to death by order of Elijah.

Pagan Theatrics: Interestingly, such contests or "theatrics" were often used by the priests of other religions. They would "fight" against evil, invoking one of their gods for assistance. Often, appearing to fail, and just before succumbing to the evil, the priest would be "rescued" or "comforted" by a very beautiful virgin woman. With renewed strength and confidence, the priest would then rally and defeat the evil. The theatrics concluded with the priest and the beautiful woman going off "into the sunset" to consummate their victory. Often the people returned home with a souvenir—a small replica of the woman representing a goddess of fertility. The souvenir may have been ugly, but it reminded the bearer of the vicarious "arousing" experience just witnessed. This type of religious prostitution was abhorrent to the God of Israel. The people thought they could be religious and still visit the titillating dramas. In modern times the amazing similarity can be recognized in basic screenplays of James Bond, or other thrillers. As in the past, most still do not consider this to be "idol practice."

Chapter 3

Armageddon and The Highway of The Patriarchs

Megiddo and the Jezreel Valley

 Megiddo and Armageddon: Along the Way of the Sea, various mounds or tels mark ancient caravan stops or toll stations. Such mounds provided a military high ground to secure the highways. The most strategic area in the country was the Jezreel Valley with its largest tel, Megiddo. Some people feel that Megiddo and the word Armageddon are associated. In Hebrew the word for "hill" or "tel" is *har*, and the prominent har in this valley is Megiddo. Thus it became known as the valley by the Har Megiddo. Mishnaic Hebrew scholars called it "Har Megiddon."

"When messianic hope again turns cold, will Joseph's role again unfold?"

Later it became known as Armageddon. It is the connecting point of the Crossroads of the East, known by Christians as a place specified as Armageddon in the last days.

Ancient Highways: The Way of the Sea along the Mediterranean Coast approaches this valley from the west; the King's Highway along the Jordan Valley comes from the east; the Patriarchs' Highway along the north-south mountain ridge comes from the south through the middle of Israel. Let's take a short journey from the midpoint of this valley on the Patriarchs' Highway as it begins its southward, mountain route. The southern end of this highway spills into the Negev and subsequently the Sinai Desert. Virtually every army that has been in the Middle East has had a battle in this valley. They hoped to control the highways connecting great nations of the north and of the south. That is what brings us to call it the battlefield of the Crossroads of the East.

The Battle of Armageddon

Final Battle and Two Prophets: In latter days, as the nations of the world turn against the nation of Israel, a part of the final battle may again be fought here. The conflict will be delayed for three and a half years by the influence of two prophets. They will have enough political, military, and spiritual influence to hold back the armies of two hundred million people. (Armies of more than three hundred million people were gathered for the Gulf War.) Then the confrontation will break into war, killing the prophets who will lie in the streets for three and a half days. The battle will leave so many dead that it will take seven months to find and bury them. Scriptures

Watchtowers on hilltops were a common sight in ancient Israel. They were used as lookouts for enemies that might approach unseen without the tower's high vantage point. The Savior often used them to symbolize the need to guard against evil.

indicate that two-thirds of Jerusalem's population and one-third of the entire country's population will perish. The leftover instruments of war will provide the survivors with enough fuel for seven years.

Gog and the Valley of Hamon-gog:

> *And they that dwell in the cities of Israel shall go forth, and shall set on fire and burn the weapons, both the shields and the bucklers, the bows and the arrows, and the hand-staves, and the spears, and they shall burn them with fire seven years:*

> *So that they shall take no wood out of the field, neither cut down any out of the forests; for they shall burn the weapons with fire: and they shall spoil those that spoiled them, and rob those that robbed them, saith the Lord GOD.*

> *And it shall come to pass in that day, that I will give unto Gog a place there of graves in Israel, the valley of the passengers on the east of the sea: and it shall stop the noses of the passengers: and there shall they bury Gog and all his multitude: and they shall call it The valley of Hamon-gog.*

> *And seven months shall the house of Israel be burying of them, that they may cleanse the land.* EZEKIEL 39:9-12

The Great Battle:

> *And it shall come to pass, that in all the land, saith the Lord, two parts therein shall be cut off and die; but the third shall be left therein.*

> *And I will bring the third part through the fire, and will refine them as silver is refined, and will try them as gold is tried: they shall call on my name, and I will hear them: I will say, It is my people: and they shall say, The Lord is my God.* ZECHARIAH 13:8-9 (see also 11, 12, 13)

> *And thus I saw the horses in the vision, and them that sat on them, having breastplates of fire, and of jacinth, and brimstone: and the heads of the horses were as the heads of lions; and out of their mouths issued fire and smoke and brimstone.*

> *By these three was the third part of men killed, by the fire, and by the smoke, and by the brimstone, which issued out of their mouths.* REVELATION 9:17-18 (see also 16:14-21)

Settlements in the Mountains

Holding the High Ground: Anciently the children of Israel crossed the Red Sea and wandered forty years in the Sinai, Negev, and Moab wildernesses. Then they settled in mountains which stretch north to south, a spine-like backbone through the middle of the land of Canaan. Later, the land was called Palestine after the Philistines.

The mountains of Israel were fertile and provided safety from the Canaanites, Philistines, and others who had settled on the lowlands. The tribes of Benjamin, Manasseh, and Ephraim lived in these mountains. The other children—or tribes—of Israel were mostly in the higher areas where they were well-suited for mountain defense.

Watchtowers and Terraces: Towers were used to watch over the land, and hedges or terraces were used to prevent the land from washing away. Mountains, watchtowers, hedges, vineyards, and orchard terraces are commonly seen throughout the land. They have been used as imagery in various parables to symbolize the scattering and gathering of Israel. For example, Isaiah identifies the vineyard as Israel. Jesus denounces the leadership of Israel and prophesies that the executorship of Israel would be given to another nation or another people.

The Restoration of Israel: Latter-day scripture describes the gathering and restoration of Israel.

> *For the vineyard of the Lord of hosts is the house of Israel, and the men of Judah his pleasant plant:...   ISAIAH 5:7 (see also 1-7)*

> *Therefore say I unto you, The kingdom of God shall be taken from you, and given to a nation bringing forth the fruits thereof. MATTHEW 21:43 (see also 33-46)*

> *And the lord of the vineyard said unto one of his servants: Go and gather together the residue of my servants, and take all the strength of mine house, which are my warriors, my young men, and they that are of middle age also among all my servants, who are the strength of mine house, save those only whom I have appointed to tarry;*

> *And go ye straightway unto the land of my vineyard, and redeem my vineyard; for it is mine;...*
> *DOCTRINE & COVENANTS 101:55-56 (see also 43-62)*

The Ancient Patriarchs

The Patriarchs' Highway: The Patriarchs' Highway has been used for close to six millennia. The first place that the ancient patriarch Abraham offered sacrifice to the Lord in Canaan was at Shechem, on this very highway.

> *And Abram passed through the land unto the place of Sichem, unto the plain of Moreh. And the Canaanite was then in the land.*

> *And the Lord appeared unto Abram, and said, Unto thy seed will I give this land: and there builded he an altar unto the Lord, who appeared unto him. GENESIS 12:6-7 (see also 1-7)*

The First Hebrew: Abraham was the first known Hebrew, and his descendants would also be known as Hebrews. In that sense, even the Arabs, descendants of Ishmael, a son of Abraham, could be considered Hebrews.

> *...and told Abram the Hebrew; for he dwelt in the plain of Mamre...   GENESIS 14:13*

Rock-terraced walls in Bethlehem attest to the abundance of stone in Israel. It seems that the more the boulders are gathered, the more plentiful they become. It is easy to see why the rock is such an important image in the Bible.

Jacob's New Name: One grandson of this first Hebrew was Jacob, who later in life received a new name, Israel. Jews are still given an "extra" or "new" name. This is the name they use for religious events such as circumcision, immersions, Bar Mitzvahs, weddings, etc. Moslems get a new name at Mecca that they must keep secret. This name is used when they approach Allah, after death. Moslems return to Mecca in behalf of relatives who have died and did not have the chance to go to Mecca themselves. Living proxies may apparently get the new name for their relatives.

A Nation's New Name: As Jacob's name changed to Israel, he was regarded as the first Israelite; and his descendants would also be known as Israelites.

> *And he said, Thy name shall be called no more Jacob, but Israel: for as a prince hast thou power with God and with men, and hast prevailed.* GENESIS 32:28

Jacob lived at Shechem where he built an altar. This is where he also dug a well that he used for himself, his children, and his cattle.

Jacob's Well

Jesus at Jacob's Well: Jacob's well was the same one that was used by a Samaritan woman some eighteen hundred years later. There she met Jesus and wondered at His offer of living water.

> *Art thou greater than our father Jacob, which gave us the well... Jesus answered and said unto her, Whosoever drinketh of this water shall thirst again: But whosoever drinketh of the water that I shall give him shall never thirst... The woman saith unto him, ...when he [the Messiah] is come, he will tell us all things. Jesus saith unto her, I that speak unto thee am he.* JOHN 4:12-26

Washings, Immersions, and Living Water: Spring water is still very important for religious Jews. The immersions and washings that Orthodox Jews continue practicing require water that comes from bedrock, from springs that are called *mayim chai-yim*, or "living water." Therefore, the Savior's role as cleanser of our souls and references to "Living Water" and the "Rock of Salvation" symbolize the act of purification. These are just two of the many Old Testament names used to refer to the expected Messiah.

Moses and the Rock: Moses neglected to teach this symbolism or acknowledge the hand of the Lord in all things when he struck the rock at Mount Horeb to provide the murmuring Israelites with water. The lesson was that the God of Israel, not Moses, provided salvation (living water). The Deliverer was "The Fountain of Living Waters" and "The Rock of Salvation." Taking credit upon himself for being their deliverer resulted in Moses not entering the promised land.

Jacob's Well. Locals continue drawing living water to this day.

Typical ancient road.

And the Lord spake unto Moses, saying,

Take the rod, and gather thou the assembly together, thou, and Aaron thy brother, and speak ye unto the rock before their eyes; and it shall give forth his water, and thou shalt bring forth to them water out of the rock: so thou shalt give the congregation and their beasts drink.

And Moses took the rod from before the Lord, as he commanded him.

And Moses and Aaron gathered the congregation together before the rock, and he said unto them, Hear now, ye rebels; must we fetch you water out of this rock?

And Moses lifted up his hand, and with his rod he smote the rock twice: and the water came out abundantly, and the congregation drank, and their beasts also.

And the Lord spake unto Moses and Aaron, Because ye believed me not, to sanctify me in the eyes of the children of Israel, therefore ye shall not bring this congregation into the land which I have given them.   NUMBERS 20:7-12

Joseph

Joseph Becomes a Slave: Jacob's well is close to the parcel of ground given to Joseph, the eleventh son of Jacob and the firstborn son of Rachel. Joseph was chosen and appointed by his father as the executor of the family. Joseph did not continue living in Shechem. He was sold into Egypt's slave market. It seemed as if he were doomed forever to be a servant. The Hebrew word for slave is "OBED." OBED is also used as the word for servant, worker and worship! Worshipping is working and serving our God. In a sense, it is like being a slave to Him because He has paid for us. It was according to God's plan; chosen Joseph became a slave and, eventually, a servant to Pharaoh. He was to learn what the Savior later would teach,

> *But he that is greatest among you shall be your servant.*
> *MATTHEW 23:11*

Joseph Saves His Family: As a servant to Pharaoh, Joseph was in a high position to save Egypt from famine. Three years into the famine, the Israelite brothers came to Egypt seeking "foreign aid." At first, Joseph did not reveal himself. He even incarcerated his brothers for three days and nights.

> *Send one of you, and let him fetch your brother, and ye shall be kept in prison, that your words may be proved, whether there be any truth in you: or else by the life of Pharaoh surely ye are spies.*
>
> *And he put them all together into ward three days.*
> *GENESIS 42:16-17 (See also chapters 42-45)*

He then saved his family by providing them with grain. After Joseph had replenished their resources, he revealed his identity in a private family gathering. The Jewish tradition is that the brothers recognized him only after he identified himself three times.

An ancient well near Dothan, the home of youthful Joseph. It was near this place that Joseph was placed into a well and sold as a slave. From here the saga of Joseph in Egypt began.

Then Joseph could not refrain himself before all them that stood by him; and he cried, Cause every man to go out from me. And there stood no man with him, while Joseph made himself known unto his brethren.

And he wept aloud: and the Egyptians and the house of Pharaoh heard.

And Joseph said unto his brethren, I am Joseph; doth my father yet live? And his brethren could not answer him; for they were troubled at his presence.

And Joseph said unto his brethren, Come near to me, I pray you. And they came near. And he said, I am Joseph your brother, whom ye sold into Egypt.   GENESIS 45:1-4

Joseph, Son of Joseph: There are several Israelite traditions that say Joseph taught his brothers that the entire saga of being a slave, serving and saving his family, symbolized the plan of God. Jewish tradition suggests that he apparently prophesied that another Joseph in latter days would be in position to save Israel again. In the early 1900s, Rabbi Abraham HaCohen Kook was asked if the temple could now be built. He responded by suggesting that Israel would have to wait until the priestly functions would be restored. He referred to a "Messiach ben Joseph (a Joseph, son of Joseph) ... to him will be given the keys of the gathering of Israel, he will restore temple worship."

A New Home in Egypt: Due to the famine that apparently stretched throughout the Middle East, the ancient Joseph provided a new home for his family in Egypt. While Joseph was alive, and for some time thereafter, they prospered. Then, as if God needed to teach them a great eternal lesson, about four hundred years later the Israelites became servants and then slaves in bondage.

> *...there arose up a new king over Egypt, which knew not Joseph.*
> *EXODUS 1:8 (see also GENESIS 45)*

Jewish Hope for Another Joseph: As mentioned, Jewish legends persist with a hope of a latter-day Joseph, one who would receive the keys of the gathering of Israel and restore temple worship. The account of Joseph is truly symbolic. An ancient Joseph saves his family from famine; a modern Joseph is anticipated to save Israel from a spiritual famine.

Joseph's Tomb: Centuries later, another Israelite-turned-Egyptian named Moses delivered the Israelites from bondage. At that time, Joseph's bones were returned to the land of his father. In the shadow of nearby Mount Gerizim, Joseph's tomb is still used for worship. Annually, descendants of the ancient Samaritans, who were at odds with the Jews, still offer animal sacrifices. They feel that they are descendants of Joseph through his son Ephraim as well as from Levi through Aaron. In that way, through both priestly lineage and birthright, they believe themselves to be the salvation of Israel in latter days.

Joseph in Egypt: The chronicle of history with Joseph in Egypt is a chiasmus, an inverted repetition. The following poem is a chiastic image of the life and mission of Joseph, both in the past and in the future.

A Reflection of Joseph — From Judah

Our younger brother, the little one,
became our father's birthright son.
He told us he was the "chosen,"
we listened not—our hearts were frozen.
His dreams to us—a silly story,
not to him would we give glory.
And so one day our peace to save,
he was sold to become a slave.
He went away, we did not care,
his birthright lot we now would share.
We told our father a well-planned lie—
our brother, Joseph, by beast did die.
Father grieved, we hid our shame.
No more thought we to hear his name.
From us was hid the heavenly plan,
our Joseph became a mighty man.
In God's own way the plan was laid,
from us the plight would not be stayed.
Hunger and thirst we did name,
but memory was still the shame.
In Israel's land the dust did fly,
"One" must save us lest we die.
We went to Egypt to ask her share,
a ruler there for us did care.
Our brother, Joseph, once a slave,
now his brothers he did save.
To him we now did give the glory.
Our children would repeat the story.
When messianic hope again turns cold,
will Joseph's role again unfold?
Come brother, birthright son—
lead us to the Holy One.

— Daniel Rona

Chapter 4

Jezreel Valley and Northward

Jezreel Valley Reclaimed

 From Swamp to Breadbasket: Returning to the north end of the Highway of the Patriarchs', the Jezreel Valley, one must realize that as recently as the 1920s it was a malaria-infested, stinking swamp. Now, however, it is the breadbasket of Israel, producing as many as seven or eight crops a year. The most commanding view of this valley is from the top of Mount Tabor.

Looking over the now-fruitful valley, the late LDS President Harold B. Lee suggested that the valley was fertile because of the multitudes who gave their lives in battle. In that sense, symbolically, life went down into the ground in the past, and now in the present is coming back up. It has become a pleasant place, in contrast to what it was like at the beginning of the twentieth century.

"Jesus commanded them to keep it secret. What occurred may have been too sacred to repeat to just anyone."

Pleasant Grove, Nain

Raised from the Dead: In this valley is a town named Pleasant, the Naim or Nain of New Testament times, where Jesus encountered a very unpleasant situation. A widow was about to bury her only son. Jesus stopped the procession and raised the young man from death.

> *And it came to pass the day after, that he went into a city called Nain; and many of his disciples went with him, and much people.*
>
> *Now when he came nigh to the gate of the city, behold, there was a dead man carried out, the only son of his mother, and she was a widow: and much people of the city was with her.*
>
> *And when the Lord saw her, he had compassion on her, and said unto her, Weep not.*
>
> *And he came and touched the bier: and they that bare him stood still. And he said, Young man, I say unto thee, Arise.*

And he that was dead sat up, and began to speak. And he delivered him to his mother.

And there came a fear on all: and they glorified God, saying, That a great prophet is risen up among us; and, That God hath visited his people.

And this rumour of him went forth throughout all Judaea, and throughout all the region round about.   LUKE 7:11-17

Mount Tabor

The village of Nain lies opposite of the base of a dome-shaped mount named Tabor. The mountain rises majestically above the area given to the tribe of Issachar.

Issachar's Blessing: Issachar was blessed by his father, Israel. In that blessing, he called Issachar a donkey crouched with burden. The metaphor symbolizes the gathering of a harvest in a fruitful valley. An aerial view of Issachar's area even looks like the outline of a donkey with two baskets on either side. On a more humorous note, the patriarch Israel laid hands on his son's head and gave him a simple blessing, calling him

> *...a strong ass...   GENESIS 49:14*

Today calling someone a donkey is a curse. However, it was then considered a compliment! The faithful, hard-working donkey is the beast of burden bringing in the harvest. Wealth and well-being was Issachar's real blessing.

Traditional Transfiguration Site: A short distance across the valley is Mount Tabor. Many feel that Mount Tabor is the site of the transfiguration is strongest. However, some feel that Mount Hermon in the very north of Galilee, by Caesarea Philippi, might be the site. The late LDS President Spencer W. Kimball related a very personal experience about Mount Tabor in 1979. You could sense that he felt that Tabor was the transfiguration location as he said, "I felt like I was on the highest spot on the face of the earth." In talking about his experience, he quoted the verses from Matthew:

> *...Jesus taketh Peter, James, and John his brother, and bringeth them up into an high mountain apart,   MATTHEW 17:1*

Then a bright cloud overshadowed them as Jesus was wondrously transfigured, and the voice of God was heard,

> *This is my beloved Son, in whom I am well pleased...*
> *MATTHEW 17:5 (see also 1-9)*

Not only was Jesus transfigured, but Moses and Elijah also appeared. Peter, James, and John experienced what the Jews had long awaited: the return of Moses and Elijah. Some see this as a symbolic pivotal point, the passing of the priesthood keys from the old prophets to the new apostles on Mount Tabor. Physically, Mount Tabor could be seen as a pivotal point between the Old Testament (mostly southward) and the New Testament (mostly northward). As profound as this experience was, Jesus commanded them to keep it secret. What occurred may have been too sacred to repeat to just anyone.

The traditional place of the Transfiguration of Jesus, Mount Tabor is also the site where Deborah and Barak gathered before defeating Sisera.

Another interesting consideration is the question Peter posed to Jesus,

> *...it is good for us to be here: if thou wilt, let us make here three tabernacles; one for thee, and one for Moses, and one for Elias [Elijah].*   MATTHEW 17:4

The Feast of the Tabernacles: The season of this remarkable event places it late summer or early autumn, close to the Jewish Feast of Tabernacles (Sukkot). That is when observant Jews build temporary tabernacles (booths) to live in for a week. They celebrate the deliverance of Israel from Egypt and the "temporary housing" the Israelites experienced in their wilderness journey. During this week, the door is left open for the awaited arrival of expected biblical guests, including Elijah and Moses. Imagine the thrill of the Apostles upon seeing the ancient prophets at the seasonal holiday when they were expected!

Nazareth

Childhood Home of Jesus: Well off the traditional crossroad is Nazareth. Today it is a busy city of Arabs and Jews. Its Arab population makes it one of the largest Arab cities in Israel. About twelve hundred feet above sea level and halfway between the Mediterranean and the waters of Galilee, this obscure town became the childhood home of Jesus. His upbringing surely included learning the tasks and crafts of his environment.

> *Is not this the carpenter's son?...*   MATTHEW 13:55

Although western language Bibles refer to Mary's husband, Joseph, as a carpenter, the Greek Bible (the New Testament was originally compiled in Greek), calls him a craftsman. The industry of Nazareth was, and still is, the regional rock quarry.

Rock of Salvation: That profession surely would have included the trade of working in stone. Interestingly, Jehovah, later known as Jesus, is called the "Rock of Salvation."

> *The God of my rock; in him will I trust: he is my shield, and the horn of my salvation, my high tower, and my refuge, my saviour; thou savest me from violence.*   2 SAMUEL 22:3

Although it is popular to consider Jesus as a carpenter, one can easily see that he also studied the Law of Moses. In fact, he was considered a rabbi, one schooled in the law. At twelve years of age he was in the temple, with the lawyers, answering and asking questions. Was this an apprentice craftsman or an apprentice lawyer becoming a "son of the law" (*Bar Mitzvah* in Aramaic)? Nowadays, someone schooled in the law is called a lawyer. After all, Jesus was the lawgiver, our advocate with the Father.

> *For the Lord is our judge, the Lord is our lawgiver, the Lord is our king; he will save us.*   ISAIAH 33:22

Bar Mitzvah: When a Jewish lad turns twelve years of age, he has the opportunity to study a section of the Law and the Prophets, a section he will recite at his Bar Mitzvah. Jews regularly read the Law and the Prophets publicly three times a week (Mondays, Thursdays, and Saturday-Sabbaths). All congregations read the same section on each of those days. Therefore, the boy must choose which day he will

First century ruins still exist in Nazareth.

read—and then be trained in that particular section throughout his twelfth year. A lawyer (rabbi) has been sufficiently trained to read the appropriate sections at any given time. Jesus apparently had that training.

> *And he came to Nazareth, where he had been brought up: and, as his custom was, he went into the synagogue on the sabbath day, and stood up for to read.* LUKE 4:16

Messianic Prophecy: Jesus concluded by testifying that he was the fulfillment of Isaiah's messianic prophecy.

> *And there was delivered unto him the book of the prophet Esaias. And when he had opened the book, he found the place where it was written,*
>
> *The Spirit of the Lord is upon me, because he hath anointed me to preach the gospel to the poor; he hath sent me to heal the broken-hearted, to preach deliverance to the captives, and recovering of sight to the blind, to set at liberty them that are bruised,*
>
> *To preach the acceptable year of the Lord.*
>
> *And he closed the book, and he gave it again to the minister, and sat down. And the eyes of all them that were in the synagogue were fastened on him.*
>
> *And he began to say unto them, This day is this scripture fulfilled in your ears.* LUKE 4:17-21

The congregation became enraged that he would appoint himself as the "Anointed One" (*Messiah* in Hebrew). To them, that kind of blasphemy warranted death!

> *And all they in the synagogue, when they heard these things, were filled with wrath,*
>
> *And rose up, and thrust him out of the city, and led him unto the brow of the hill whereon their city was built, that they might cast him down headlong.* LUKE 4:28-29

Mount of Precipitation

The Jezreel valley, the "Crossroads of the East" that Christians call "Armageddon." Just prior to the establishment of the State of Israel, Jews drained the rotten swamps creating the bread basket of new Israel.

Close to forty different churches mark traditional sites of Jesus' youth. However, the only scripturally-supported site is an old Nazareth quarry.

A Place for Stoning: This is probably the place where angered Nazarenes would have stoned Jesus for blasphemy. It is known today as the Mount of Jumping or the Mount of Precipitation. Rabbinic interpretations of the ancient Jewish law of stoning indicate that it was required that the victim be thrown over a cliff (the execution). The accuser was responsible to make sure the criminal was dead. The accuser always had to cast the first stone, and then others threw stones to cover the body (the burial). Jesus was brought to the edge of the hill,

> *But he passing through the midst of them went his way,* LUKE 4:30

Hills of Galilee

The Sea of Galilee: Eastward from Nazareth, the peaceful Sea of Galilee lies 700 feet below sea level. It is surrounded by hills and the eastern Golan mountains with Mount Hermon rising majestically 9,232 feet above sea level. Having been rejected at Nazareth, Jesus spent most of his ministry in towns surrounding this lake.

A Hebrew Harp: The shape of the lake is like a harp; in old Hebrew a harp was probably called a *kinor*, and thus another name for the lake is Kinneret, quite possibly derived from the word kinor. In the northward hills lived the ancient tribe of Naphtali and the tribe of Dan.

> *...to the children of Naphtali, even for the children of Naphtali according to their families.*
>
> *And their coast was from Heleph, from Allon to Zaanannim, and Adami, Nekeb, and Jabneel, unto Lakum; and the outgoings thereof were at Jordan:*
>
> *And then the coast turneth westward to Aznoth-tabor, and goeth out from thence to Hukkok, and reacheth to Zebulun on the south side, and reacheth to Asher on the west side, and to Judah upon Jordan toward the sunrising.*
>
> *And the fenced cities are Ziddim, Zer, and Hammath, Rakkath, and Chinnereth,*
>
> *And Adamah, and Ramah, and Hazor,*
>
> *And Kedesh, and Edrei, and En-hazor,*
>
> *And Iron, and Migdal-el, Horem, and Beth-anath, and Beth-shemesh; nineteen cities with their villages.*
>
> *This is the inheritance of the tribe of the children of Naphtali according to their families, the cities and their villages.*   *JOSHUA 19:32-39*
>
> *And they called the name of the city Dan, after the name of Dan their father, who was born unto Israel: howbeit the name of the city was Laish at the first.*   *JUDGES 18:29*

The surrounding hills tower over a Bedouin tent on the shores of the Sea of Galilee. The steep hillsides and mountains surrounding the lake cause a wide range of temperatures that can often precipitate sudden violent storms.

Hazor

The Largest Tel in Israel: At the base of the hills of Naphtali is the largely manmade mound of Hazor. It is the largest tel in the country and has had as many as forty thousand inhabitants living there at one time. One of its twenty levels of civilization covered close to two hundred acres. Hazor was one of the three main tels or fortified cities that Solomon used to govern the country of Israel.

> *And this is the reason of the levy which king Solomon raised; for to build the house of the Lord, and his own house, and Millo, and the wall of Jerusalem, and Hazor, and Megiddo, and Gezer.*   *1 KINGS 9:15*

*In contrast to modern Israel,
Bedouin still live in tents.*

Hazor's Ancient Role: Megiddo governed the middle area, and Gezer was the headquarters over the southern area of Israel. Hazor in the north was the main taxation control center for the northern third of the land and people of Israel. An archaeological discovery included a temple with covenant altars depicting two hands and arms in an upright position in an attitude of prayer. A sacrificial altar was also found with points or "horns" on the four corners of the altar. This temple was nearly identical to two other temples found at Megiddo and Gezer.

Kibbutz Kfar Giladi

A Collective Settlement: Close to Israel's northern-most town of Metulla is Kibbutz Kfar Giladi. Established almost seventy years ago, this agricultural collective settlement has close to seven hundred members. They farm, milk their hundreds of cows three times daily, operate the largest rock quarries in Israel, manufacture eyeglass frames, and cater a lovely guest hotel. This is typical of the close to three hundred different kibbutz settlements throughout Israel. *Kibbutzniks* make up only about three percent of the population, yet they produce close to 75 percent of the food Israel consumes. Additionally, they are greatly involved in agricultural exports sent throughout the world.

A Modern United Order: The motivation of a kibbutz is based on a united order of work and family life—dedicated to the good of all in the kibbutz. Most of the kibbutzim are usually not religious, although one of the four kibbutz federations is specifically Orthodox. (There are about two dozen such religious kibbutzim.) All activities are oriented to overall needs, as decided by the social and democratic judgment of the kibbutz community. Education follows the standards of Israel's Ministry of Education. Primary grades are usually kibbutz based, teenagers join high schools in the community, and at age eighteen they join the military. There they have the same opportunities as other citizens.

Military Service: Kibbutz members are citizens of Israel, and all Israeli citizens including Druze and Bedouin, serve in the military. Women are still assigned a minimum of twenty months and men a minimum of thirty-six months of service. The ultra-religious women are totally exempt, and some of the ultra-religious men serve in *yeshivas* (institutes of religion). These special yeshivas do have some military training that supplements religious training. Throughout Israel, Arabs are not required to serve in the military services.

Security in Israel: Israel pays close attention to its security. A closer look reveals that Israel is a good land where Jews, Moslems, and Christians can raise their families; a land along the Mediterranean where ancient Jaffa and Caesarea lie; a land where Nazareth and the Galilee are nestled in mountains; a land green from water (there are the "Med," the Red, and the Dead Seas)! Israel's peaceful countryside reflects less than two generations of hard-working pioneers—a new Israel in an ancient homeland.

SCRIPTURAL REFERENCES (KJV)

Section One

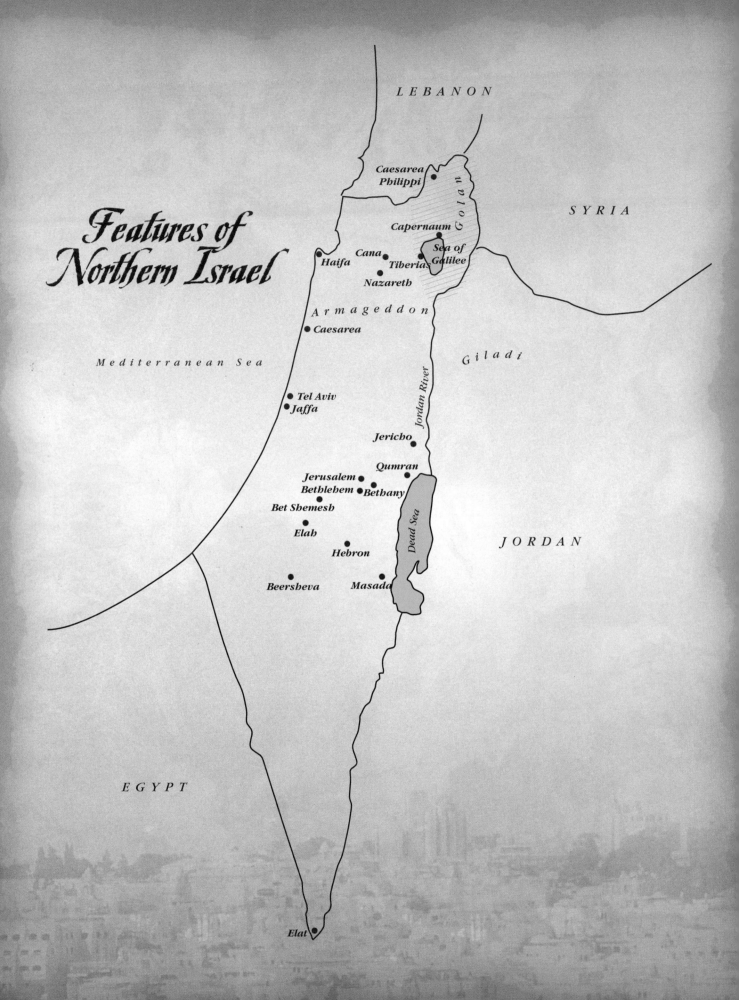

Features of Northern Israel

LEBANON

SYRIA

Caesarea Philippi

Golan

Capernaum

Cana

Haifa · Tiberias

Sea of Galilee

Nazareth

Armageddon

Caesarea

Mediterranean Sea

Giladi

Jordan River

Tel Aviv
Jaffa

Jericho

Qumran

Jerusalem

Bethlehem · Bethany

Bet Shemesh

Dead Sea

JORDAN

Elah

Hebron

Beersheva · Masada

EGYPT

Elat

~ *Overview* ~
Galilee

LEBANON'S BORDER AREA with Israel was once a malaria-infested swamp that has now turned fruitfully beautiful. Starting at **TEL DAN** is one of the major springs forming the upper **JORDAN RIVER**. Water, cold and pure, bursts out of the ground. A few miles further is the **BANIAS**, also known as **CAESAREA PHILIPPI**, which is another source of the Jordan River that flows into the **SEA OF GALILEE**. In the **GOLAN HEIGHTS** are many Druze villages as well as relics of old Syrian bunkers, silent since the 1967 Six-Day War with Israel. Descending the Heights, one can see another breathtaking view of the **SEA OF GALILEE**. Nearby are the famous ruins of the first-century town of **CAPERNAUM**, where Jesus did most of his miracles. The peaceful **MOUNT OF BEATITUDES** is also on this northern shore. On this hill, a quiet, spirit-filled spot overlooks the sea where many wonders occurred. **TIBERIAS** is the site of Herod's ancient hot springs resort. Our study route skirts the western shore of the **SEA OF GALILEE**. Then it follows along the lower **JORDAN RIVER** as it continues its journey. Leaving the southern shores of the lake, it meanders through the Jordan River Rift to the lowest spot on the face of the earth, the **DEAD SEA**.

*Fishermen begin work early on the Sea of Galilee
and sometimes fish all night. Jesus walked on the
water to a boat on this lake and preached some
of his sermons from its shores. The Apostle Peter
was a fisherman on the Sea of Galilee.*

Chapter 5

The Golan

Hills of Naphtali

 Overlooking the Galilee: For me, the thought of the Golan imparts a peaceful feeling. I enjoy its beauty and majesty. Overlooking the Hula Valley and the Sea of Galilee, Israel's northern border forms a panhandle that is less than ten miles wide from east to west. The hills of Naphtali run north and south and form a western border between Israel and Lebanon. In ancient days, the tribe of Naphtali lived in this fertile region. The eastern border is made up by the Golan Heights. Northern Golan is where the ancient tribe of Dan lived. The tops of the hills of Naphtali and the northern part of the Golan Heights border the now peaceful southern Lebanon.

Lebanon and Israel

Chaos in Lebanon: Up to the 1980s, the Lebanese civil wars and conflicts were stirred up by the anarchy of the PLO and other terrorist groups. Southern Lebanon became isolated. When Israel was proclaimed a state in 1948, many Arabs from Israel's north settled permanently in southern Lebanon. They were then just over the border of Israel. Recently, thousands of these same Moslems and Christians have come back across Israel's "Good Fence" for medical aid and to shop for basic necessities.

Lebanese Workers in Israel: Unbeknown to most people, up to the year 2000, there were hundreds of Lebanese that regularly worked in Israel. Some even drove their cars, specially licensed, back and forth across the border. There was an unofficial currency exchange that was so stable that these Lebanese workers got paid in Israel with Lebanese currency. Unfortunately, there is an ever-perpetuating gang mentality that has spawned newer groups of terrorists in southern Lebanon. Slowly, the new Lebanese government is weeding out these groups, and Lebanon may have a chance to return to its former beauty.

The Beauty of Lebanon: In the past, Lebanon was referred to as the "Switzerland of the Middle East." The snow-capped mountains and financial facilities attracted the elite of the region. The skiing for which Lebanon was well known has now shifted to Mount Hermon in Israel. The new peace movements with Israel's neighbors also signal a great financial future, as the economies rejuvenate and trade flourishes as it did anciently. Times were good in the past, but conflicts reduced the area's resources and grandeur to swamps and impoverishment.

"The people truly expected a healing, and yet Jesus knew that was only part of the real purpose. He had a whole lesson in mind."

The Hula Valley

Fertile Land from the Swamps: The challenge to drain the stinking swamps, called the Hula, was met by new Jewish immigrants in the 1940s and 50s. The land is abundantly fruitful again. Now that the borders have opened, many returning Lebanese visitors are surprised to see the new landscape. It has changed considerably since they last saw it almost forty years ago. New settlements and development towns like Metulla, Kfar Giladi and Kiryat Shemona dot the fertile countryside.

Metulla and Kibbutz Kfar Giladi: Metulla is the northernmost city in Israel. It is best known for its frontier opening into Lebanon called the "Good Fence." Metulla is like a ski village with alpine-like hotels. The spirit of identity is high, as residents have maintained the security of northern Israel by preserving their farms and homes along Israel's northern border. Nearby, Kibbutz Kfar Giladi began in 1916, and is a typical agricultural collective settlement, as well as a popular tourist hotel with vacation facilities. A very brief lesson in Hebrew helps us understand the meaning of the word *kfar*; it means a "small town" or "village." A man named Gilad was one of the founders of the kibbutz; they honored him by naming it Kfar Giladi.

City of Eight: Next to the kibbutz is the city of Kiryat Shemona. In Hebrew, the word *kiryat* denotes the word "city" and the word *shemona* denotes the word "eight." Kiryat Shemona is named after eight men who defended this area in the War of Independence. Unbeknown to their Arab attackers, the eight men were mortally wounded but fought so ferociously before they died that the attackers fell back and abandoned their efforts. As an honor to the eight fallen Jews, the new Israeli city was named City of Eight, Kiryat Shemona.

The Springs of the Jordan

Sources of the Jordan River: Much of the fertility of this region comes from the luscious nature preserve bursting forth with springs, trickles, and bubbling brooks. The three sources of the Jordan River that come together are from the Lebanese mountains, Mount Hermon (Banias), and the springs of Dan. A walk through the Dan area is like a stroll in the Garden of Eden. The waters depart from the ruins of the tribe of Dan and combine with the runoff from Mount Hermon, then flow down to the Sea of Galilee. The Hebrew word for "going down" is *yored*. Some people feel that the term or expression yored-Dan is the origin of the name Jordan (although Joshua crossed the Jordan River before the tribe of Dan had settled in this northern area). It is quite possible that the account, written later, simply used the then-known word "Jordan."

The Ancient Resort of Banias: *Banias* as a name is derived from the name *Paneus*, meaning a "place" and "resort" where the mythological god Pan was worshiped. Incidentally, in Greek/Roman mythology, the god Pan was responsible for nature and vegetation. The Romans held pagan worship activities in this extraordinary, verdant area. The cultic religion was a nature adulation, probably in

A young boy receives a blessing by the laying-on-of-hands during his Bar Mitzvah celebration at the Western Wall in Jerusalem. The similarity of the form of this blessing to a Priesthood blessing is striking.

Caesarea Philippi is situated at the foot of Mount Hermon, and was built by Philip the tetrarch to honor Augustus Caesar. It was here that Jesus changed Simon's name to Peter – the rock.

a natural state of being. It may be part of an apostasy of ancient nature worship called Groves.

> *And they left the house of the Lord God of their fathers, and served groves and idols: and wrath came upon Judah and Jerusalem for this their trespass.* 2 CHRONICLES 24:18

Caesarea Philippi

Prominent Roman City: At the foot of Mount Hermon, where the Banias source of the Jordan River begins and by a huge rock escarpment, stood the two-thousand-year-old town of Caesarea Philippi built by Herod Philip. Recent excavations are revealing a once-prominent Roman city. The Jewish inhabitants lived on the periphery or edge of town. The New Testament account of this city begins with the words,

> *When Jesus came into the coasts of Caesarea Philippi...*
> MATTHEW 16:13

The Greek rendition of the English word *coasts* really means "border" or "edge" of town. Here, Jesus asked his disciples,

> *...Whom do men say that I the Son of man am?*
>
> [And then] *...whom say ye that I am.* MATTHEW 16:13, 15

Simon Becomes a Rock: Simon, son of Jonah (*Bar Jonah* in Aramaic means the "son of your father Jonah"), answered,

> *...Thou art the Christ, the Son of the living God.*
> MATTHEW 16:16 (see also 13-19)

Jesus responded to Simon by calling him Peter (*Cephas* in Hebrew, *Petrus* in Greek, meaning a "rock"). Peter could be "Rocky" in very modern English.

Rock of Revelation: Jesus, most likely indicating the massive rock, reminded Simon Peter that flesh and blood had not revealed it to him, but that his Father in Heaven had. The dialogue had words from the Hebrew, Aramaic, and possibly Greek languages. Here is a lesson for Simon Peter (and all of us). There is a difference between perceiving things by man's understanding (flesh and blood) and perceiving things through revelation (from his Father in Heaven). The word play extends to us today; a sure way to recognize the Messiah, the Son of the Living God, is with the rock of revelation.

The Druze

Descendants of Jethro: On Mount Hermon in the Golan Heights are several villages of Druze, a people claiming to be descendants of Jethro, the father-in-law of Moses. Jethro was a Midianite. They may be descendants of Keturah, one of Abraham's concubines, who had six sons.

Then again Abraham took a wife, and her name was Keturah.

And she bare him Zimran, and Jokshan, and Medan, and Midian, and Ishbak, and Shuah.   GENESIS 25:1-2

Druze Industry and Religion: The Druze' industrious nature and secretive religious functions, customs, and traditions make them an unusual and colorful people. They are an integral part of Israel's modern population, serving in government and military positions.

The Druze and Syria: Probably half of the Druze people still live in Syria. Israel has made repeated efforts to open the Syrian border for family reunification. This is slowly happening, as various face-saving actions are done by the Israeli Druze. They somewhat manipulate the media in publicly proclaiming Syria as mentors of the Druze people. The Druze are apparently publicly giving up Israeli identification to please the Syrians. These annual demonstrations are usually held on Syria's national holiday. Since the media has picked up these apparent protests, hundreds of Druze have crossed back and forth across the borders. I call it a "Druze Ruse." This will probably continue as long as the media does not publicize the crossings.

The Kenites

Some speculation suggests that the Druze may be much like the ancient biblical Kenite people, who, unlike the Canaanites, were loyal to Israel.

And Saul said unto the Kenites, Go, depart, get you down from among the Amalekites, lest I destroy you with them: for ye shewed kindness to all the children of Israel, when they came up out of Egypt.   So the Kenites departed from among the Amalekites.
1 SAMUEL 15:6

Temple Builders: Modern archaeology seems to reveal that the Kenites practiced similar Israelite religious customs and even built their temples like the Temple of Israel. (Their temples also had three courtyards, a holy of holies, a horned altar, etc.)

Golan Heights

Ancient Inhabitants of the Golan: The Golan was inhabited by Israel and, as mentioned before, specifically by the tribe of Dan. A part of the tribe of Manasseh and some Levites lived in the Golan in Old Testament times as well.

And unto the children of Gershon, of the families of the Levites, out of the other half tribe of Manasseh they gave Golan in Bashan with her suburbs, to be a city of refuge for the slayer; and Beeshterah with her suburbs; two cities.   JOSHUA 21:27

Most of the New Testament accounts of Jesus' ministry occurred in the Golan/Galilee area. Capernaum, Chorazin, and Bethsaida lie at the foothills of the Golan.

Golan Agriculture: Since 1967, the Golan has become a peaceful place. Israelis have cleared this rocky land and discovered great farming soil and new water sources. The unique combination of rich volcanic soil and modern farming techniques has produced outstanding agricultural yields, including award-winning grape and wine production for modern Israel.

Close to sixty different ancient Jewish sites, dating to the third, fourth, and fifth centuries after Jesus, were found, as new Jewish settlements were established.

Troubled Past of the Golan: During the first two decades of the modern State of Israel, it was obvious that the Syrians had only used the Golan for firing on Israeli settlements in the Hula Valley and around the Sea of Galilee. The one city the Syrians had, called Qunietra, was returned; but the Syrians have not repopulated or rebuilt it for more than three decades. Recent peace overtures throughout the Middle East have prompted Israel to suggest a return of the Golan in exchange for a peace treaty. Other neighboring countries have already agreed to such compromises.

During the 1967 Six-Day War, the Israelis moved the Syrians off the western side of the heights and relegated them to the eastern lowlands on the other side. Since then, on the Israeli side, the Hula Valley and the Golan above it have become fruitful.

The Shores of Galilee

At the lower and southern end of the Golan on the eastern shore of the Sea of Galilee is a more desolate place where few people lived. During Jesus' ministry, he went there to be alone.

Loaves and Fishes: When the people heard that he was on the other side of the sea, they followed him out of their cities. He blessed them and preached to them until the disciples urged Jesus to let them go home to buy food, He said,

> *...Give ye them to eat. And they said, We have no more but five loaves and two fishes; except we should go and buy meat for all this people.*
>
> *For they were about five thousand men. And he said to his disciples, Make them sit down by fifties in a company.*
>
> *And they did so, and made them all sit down.*
>
> *Then he took the five loaves and the two fishes, and looking up to heaven, he blessed them, and brake, and gave to the disciples to set before the multitude.*
>
> *And they did eat, and were all filled: and there was taken up of fragments that remained to them twelve baskets. LUKE 9:13-17*

Jesus told the disciples to feed the people, and they said it couldn't be done because they did not have enough food. Surely five loaves and two fishes could never feed the multitude! Still, Jesus did not change his charge. He took what

The shoreline of the Sea of Galilee was the location of many important events in the life of the Savior. He often preached to the multitudes here, and called his disciples from their boats while He stood on the shore.

they had, prepared it, and returned it to the disciples. Then they fed the loaves and fishes to five thousand—not counting women or children. There was even enough left over for each disciple to have a basket of food for himself.

Capernaum

A Roman and Jewish City: In recent times, excavations have uncovered the ruins of a once-thriving city of Romans and Jews. In ancient times, Capernaum was a Roman toll station, and may have had ten thousand inhabitants.

Toll Paid by a Fish: It seems that a toll taker challenged Peter for the tribute money on his guest, Jesus of Nazareth. Peter apparently offered to pay it, but Jesus began a significant dialogue:

> *...What thinkest thou, Simon? of whom do the kings of the earth take custom or tribute? of their own children, or of strangers?*
>
> *Peter saith unto him, Of strangers. Jesus saith unto him, Then are the children free.*
>
> *Notwithstanding, lest we should offend them, go thou to the sea, and cast an hook, and take up the fish that first cometh up; and when thou hast opened his mouth, thou shalt find a piece of money: that take, and give unto them for me and thee.*
> *MATTHEW 17:25-27*

The goodwill that Jesus demonstrated is a lesson Peter was to learn. Graciously, Peter offered to pay the tribute for Jesus (which actually was unnecessary because residents did not have to pay the toll). Jesus, even more graciously, had Peter catch a fish which contained a coin in its mouth—a coin of large enough value to pay the toll for both of them.

The Home of Peter: Capernaum was the home of Peter, Andrew, and other Apostles, including James, John, and Matthew.

> *And they went into Capernaum; and straightway on the sabbath day he entered into the synagogue, and taught.*
>
> *And forthwith, when they were come out of the synagogue, they entered into the house of Simon and Andrew, with James and John. MARK 1:21, 29*

Matthew Called: As mentioned, Capernaum was a toll station on the Roman road to and from Damascus. Matthew left his profession as a toll or customs taker to become one of the apostles.

> *And as Jesus passed forth from thence, he saw a man, named Matthew, sitting at the receipt of custom: and he saith unto him, Follow me. And he arose, and followed him. MATTHEW 9:9*

Most Miracles Performed Here: Jesus lived here for eighteen to twenty months of his three-year ministry. Most of his miracles occurred here or at nearby Chorazin

or Bethsaida. Sadly, these three cities were cursed by Jesus and only their ruins are visible today.

> *Then began he to upbraid the cities wherein most of his mighty works were done, because they repented not:*
>
> *Woe unto thee, Chorazin! woe unto thee, Bethsaida! for if the mighty works, which were done in you, had been done in Tyre and Sidon, they would have repented long ago in sackcloth and ashes.*
>
> *But I say unto you, It shall be more tolerable for Tyre and Sidon at the day of judgment, than for you.*
>
> *And thou, Capernaum, which art exalted unto heaven, shalt be brought down to hell: for if the mighty works, which have been done in thee, had been done in Sodom, it would have remained until this day.*
>
> *But I say unto you, That it shall be more tolerable for the land of Sodom in the day of judgment, than for thee.*
> *MATTHEW 11:20-24*

Palsied Man Healed: Some other of the better-known miracles that happened at Capernaum include a palsied man being lowered through the roof on his bed so Jesus could heal him.

> *And they come unto him, bringing one sick of the palsy, which was borne of four.*
>
> *And when they could not come nigh unto him for the press, they uncovered the roof where he was: and when they had broken it up, they let down the bed wherein the sick of the palsy lay.*
> *MARK 2:3-4*

The people truly expected a healing, and yet Jesus knew the healing was only part of the miracle. He had a greater lesson in mind.

> *When Jesus saw their faith, he said unto the sick of the palsy, Son, thy sins be forgiven thee.*
>
> *But there were certain of the scribes sitting there, and reasoning in their hearts,*
>
> *Why doth this man thus speak blasphemies? who can forgive sins but God only?*
>
> *And immediately when Jesus perceived in his spirit that they so reasoned within themselves, he said unto them, Why reason ye these things in your hearts?*
>
> *Whether is it easier to say to the sick of the palsy, Thy sins be forgiven thee; or to say, Arise, and take up thy bed, and walk?*

A modern shepherd boy holds a lamb in his arms while on the Mount of Beatitudes.

*But that ye may know that the Son of man hath power on earth
to forgive sins, (he saith to the sick of the palsy,)*

*I say unto thee, Arise, and take up thy bed, and go thy way into
thine house.*

*And immediately he arose, took up the bed, and went forth before
them all; insomuch that they were all amazed, and glorified God,
saying, We never saw it on this fashion.   MARK 2:5-12*

Withered Hand Healed: If you look closely you can see his holistic purpose.
Another example is the healing of a man with a withered hand.

*And, behold, there was a man which had his hand withered. And
they asked him, saying, Is it lawful to heal on the sabbath days?
that they might accuse him.*

...Wherefore it is lawful to do well on the sabbath days.

*Then saith he to the man, Stretch forth thine hand. And he
stretched it forth; and it was restored whole, like as the other.
MATTHEW 12:10, 12, 13*

Healing the Soul: To many, the healings were seen as external evidences, but
surely on a personal level the Master was healing the whole soul.

*For this people's heart is waxed gross, and their ears are dull of
hearing, and their eyes they have closed; lest at any time they
should see with their eyes, and hear with their ears, and should
understand with their heart, and should be converted, and I
should heal them.   MATTHEW 13:15*

Healing Peter's Mother-in-law: Jesus' quiet power was immediate. That is
evident as he healed Peter's mother-in-law.

*And when Jesus was come into Peter's house, he saw his wife's
mother laid, and sick of a fever.*

*And he touched her hand, and the fever left her: and she arose,
and ministered unto them.   MATTHEW 8:14-15*

A Multitude of Fish: The Master's method of teaching included contrasts of
people's earthly abilities and his heavenly power. Jesus instructed Peter, an
experienced fisherman, to catch fish (after failing to catch anything all night).
Surely the thought must have crossed Peter's mind that a land person was not as
skillful as Peter's crew.

*And he entered into one of the ships, which was Simon's, and
prayed him that he would thrust out a little from the land. And he
sat down, and taught the people out of the ship.*

*Now when he had left speaking, he said unto Simon, Launch out
into the deep, and let down your nets for a draught.*

*Daniel Rona demonstrates a Talith –
A traditional religious Jewish garment.
The Talith has symbolic significance with
the number of knots and strings used as
reminders of the 613 laws and commandments given to Israel by God.*

And Simon answering said unto him, Master, we have toiled all the night, and have taken nothing: nevertheless at thy word I will let down the net.

And when they had this done, they inclosed a great multitude of fishes: and their net brake.

For he was astonished, and all that were with him, at the draught of the fishes which they had taken:

... And Jesus said... Fear not; from henceforth thou shalt catch men.

... they forsook all, and followed him.   LUKE 5:3-6, 9-11

A Centurion's Servant: To sense the personal gracious nature of Jesus' relationships, let's consider the account of a Roman centurion, whose servant was gravely ill.

Now when he had ended all his sayings in the audience of the people, he entered into Capernaum.

And a certain centurion's servant, who was dear unto him, was sick, and ready to die.

And when he heard of Jesus, he sent unto him the elders of the Jews, beseeching him that he would come and heal his servant.

And when they came to Jesus, they besought him instantly, saying, That he was worthy for whom he should do this:

For he loveth our nation, and he hath built us a synagogue.

Then Jesus went with them. And when he was now not far from the house, the centurion sent friends to him, saying unto him, Lord, trouble not thyself: for I am not worthy that thou shouldest enter under my roof:

Wherefore neither thought I myself worthy to come unto thee: but say in a word, and my servant shall be healed.

For I also am a man set under authority, having under me soldiers, and I say unto one, Go, and he goeth; and to another, Come, and he cometh; and to my servant, Do this, and he doeth it.

When Jesus heard these things, he marvelled at him, and turned him about, and said unto the people that followed him, I say unto you, I have not found so great faith, no, not in Israel.

And they that were sent, returning to the house, found the servant whole that had been sick.   LUKE 7:1-10

According to Jewish practices in those days, it was not proper for a Jew to come into the house of a foreigner. Peter reiterated that custom when he spoke to another centurion in Caesarea.

Sacred moment at Barlucci's Mount of Beatitudes Church.

...Ye know how that it is an unlawful thing for a man that is a Jew to keep company, or come unto one of another nation;...
ACTS 10:28

However, Jesus graciously acquiesced to come to the centurion's house. The Roman graciously constrained Jesus from compromising Jewish custom by asking him to bless his servant from a distance. His belief was so strong that he trusted the Savior's power in spite of circumstances. His love for the Jews was so strong that he built their meeting house. Even today, the remains of the synagogue at Capernaum reveal the Roman construction and style. Archaeology confirms the written scriptural account.

Allow the Children: Upon closer examination, we can also see the hospitable nature of Jesus' personality. He must have made many friends here; after all, thousands followed him. It is conceivable that the very first ones to gather around him when he arrived to speak were the little children. He might have had special names or nicknames for them. He called Simon Bar Jonah, Peter, a name denoting rock (maybe Simon's physique was like a rock. Later, the rock would sink, and Jesus, the Rock of Salvation, would save him.) Many parents also brought their children for blessings. The disciples attempted to turn them away so they would not disturb the Master; he responded,

...Suffer [allow] little children, and forbid them not, to come unto me: for of such is the kingdom of heaven. *MATTHEW 19:14*

Touching His Garment: Of the children at Capernaum, I recall the account of a twelve-year-old girl who was ill. Her father, the leader of the synagogue, begged Jesus to come and heal her. On the way to bless her, Jesus noted that a woman had touched his garment.

And when Jesus was passed over again by ship unto the other side, much people gathered unto him:...

And, behold, there cometh one of the rulers of the synagogue, Jairus by name; and when he saw him, he fell at his feet,

And besought him greatly, saying, My little daughter lieth at the point of death: I pray thee, come and lay thy hands on her, that she may be healed; and she shall live.

And Jesus went with him; and much people followed him, and thronged him.

And a certain woman, which had an issue of blood twelve years,

And had suffered many things of many physicians, and had spent all that she had, and was nothing bettered, but rather grew worse,

When she had heard of Jesus, came in the press behind, and touched his garment.

For she said, If I may touch but his clothes, I shall be whole.

The remains of an ancient Jewish synagogue in Capernaum shows Roman architecture. At the time of Jesus, a Roman "built us a synagogue." Capernaum was the home of Peter, the Apostle, and was the site of most of the miracles Jesus performed.

> *And straightway the fountain of her blood was dried up; and she felt in her body that she was healed of that plague.*
>
> *And Jesus, immediately knowing in himself that virtue had gone out of him, turned him about in the press, and said, Who touched my clothes?   MARK 5:21-30*

The Talith: Religious Jews today wear a garment of wool called a talith. The name seems to be derived from the Hebrew word for "lamb", *taleh*. The hem or the strings of the talith are customarily touched during Jewish religious services. The four sets of strings are knotted so that the sum of knots and strings equals 613—the number of laws and covenants including the Ten Commandments given to Moses on Mount Sinai. Modern Jews touch the strings and knots of the talith garment to remind and commit themselves to keeping the laws, thereby being blessed of God.

The woman who touched the garment of Jesus (probably the talith) was healed. When he questioned who had touched him, the woman fell at his feet and confessed, probably because it was totally against Jewish custom for a woman bleeding (ritually unclean) to touch anyone. Jesus assured her that her faith had made her whole.

> *And his disciples said unto him, Thou seest the multitude thronging thee, and sayest thou, Who touched me?*
>
> *And he looked round about to see her that had done this thing.*
>
> *But the woman fearing and trembling, knowing what was done in her, came and fell down before him, and told him all the truth.*
>
> *And he said unto her, Daughter, thy faith hath made thee whole; go in peace, and be whole of thy plague.   MARK 5:31-34*

Talitha Cumi—A Child Back to Life: By the time Jesus arrived to bless the daughter of the leader of the synagogue, she had died. The people laughed at Jesus when he said the girl was only asleep. He sent all the mourners away, then with Peter, James, and John,

> *...he taketh the father and the mother of the damsel... and entereth in where the damsel was lying.*
>
> *And he took the damsel by the hand, and said unto her, Talitha cumi....   MARK 5:40-41*

The endearing term *Talitha* may have been Jesus' way of saying "my little lamb," or "curly locks" (a nickname)—and *cumi* in Hebrew means get up.

> *And straightway the damsel arose, and walked....   MARK 5:42*

In discussing this event with my own curly-locked daughter, we mused on the tender feelings, personal nature, and poetry of Jesus. We wrote a poem together. Jesus' teaching methods are reflected in the following verses that a young curly-locked girl might have also thought two thousand years ago:

Talitha — The Reflections of a Little Girl

They said he was a stranger man,
but, I liked him right away.

The crowds lingered and followed him
but, I always heard him say:

Hello, my precious little one,
will you sit with me today?

He called me Talitha, curly locks,
... and he taught me how to pray.

When I was sick, he came to me;
but, my life had slipped away.

He told my father not to fear,
Have faith, he was heard to say.

Then, took my little hand and said:
Talitha, rise up and stay.

— Daniel Rona

Basalt rocks on the Mount of Beatitudes.

Chapter 6

The Galilee

Mount of Beatitudes

 A Peaceful Place: On the northern shore of the Sea of Galilee, on a higher elevation overlooking the sea, a higher law was given on the Mount of Beatitudes. Even ancient travelers have written in their journals of the peaceful feeling of this Mount. They have used the expression, "What a place of sweet spirit." A church designed by the Italian architect Antonio Barlucci marks the traditional location of the Sermon on the Mount. Considering the proximity of this place to other communities nearby where Jesus taught and lived (Capernaum, Chorazin, and Bethsaida), the breathtaking inspirational view, and the feelings travelers have reported throughout the centuries, this is likely the spot where Jesus shared an explanation of his mission with the Twelve Apostles.

Leading the Sheep Today: On a nearby farm with over a hundred sheep, a boy shepherd leads them out every morning and returns in the late afternoon. Leading sheep is quite common in this country. Typically there are about a dozen lead sheep, older ones from last year's flock. The shepherd usually has them marked with bells around their necks. It is common to hear the boy talk to his sheep. He calls them when it's time to move on, and that's when the lead sheep immediately respond, ringing their bells as they run towards their shepherd. The ringing noise alerts the other sheep, and then like a wave they begin to follow the others.

Ancient Temple Practice: The shepherd's model is similar to an ancient biblical temple practice. For example, in the inner courtyard of the temple, the chief priest would light a fire and burn incense to signal his readiness for a sacrifice. That would alert the twelve priests in the next courtyard to wash and ready themselves. Their signal to the congregation was the ringing of bells. The multitudes would then gather to follow the priests to participate in the ritual.

"Most of Jesus' miracles were very private and had great personal value for the recipients. We are privileged to also learn from them."

Sermon on the Mount

A Shepherd's Model: In a possible shepherd's role, Jesus, the Good Shepherd, gives the Sermon on the Mount, apparently to the twelve disciples. In turn, their mission was to teach the multitudes.

> *And seeing the multitudes, he went up into a mountain: and when he was set, his disciples came unto him:* *MATTHEW 5:1*

A Christian Guideline: The Beatitudes are often interpreted as being Christian guidelines.

> *Blessed are the poor in spirit ...they that mourn...the meek ...they which do hunger and thirst after righteousness ...Blessed are the merciful ...pure in heart ...peacemakers ...persecuted for righteousness' sake....*   MATTHEW 5:3-10 (See also 11)

Another Sermon on a Mount: However, there may be more to his intention, for another rendition of this same sermon is recorded as

> *...blessed are the poor in spirit <u>who come unto me</u>....*
> 3 NEPHI 12:3 (emphasis added)

In that sense the Sermon on the Mount is inviting all people, whether rich or poor in spirit, happy or mourning, popular or persecuted, to come unto Him. He promised,

> *Blessed are they which do hunger and thirst after righteousness: for they shall be filled.*   MATTHEW 5:6

Again, more insight can be gained through another rendition of that verse which states that those hungering and thirsting after righteousness would be filled

> *...with the Holy Ghost.*   3 NEPHI 12:6

Law of Moses Fulfilled: Jesus indicated that the Law of Moses was fulfilled in him, that he was restoring a higher law, one that was governed and dictated more by the spirit and intent than by the letter of the law, which was given at Mount Sinai. A better understanding of the Sermon on the Mount comes when comparing it to the "sermon" and the commandments given on Mount Sinai. For example,

> *For I say unto you, That except your righteousness shall exceed the righteousness of the scribes and Pharisees, ye shall in no case enter into the kingdom of heaven.*

> *Ye have heard that it was said by them of old time, Thou shalt not kill; and whosoever shall kill shall be in danger of the judgment:*

> *But I say unto you, That whosoever is angry with his brother... shall be in danger of the judgment:...*   MATTHEW 5:20-22

Additional Commandments: A closer look at the Beatitudes reveals that Jesus gave additional commandments. They were based on the original Law of Moses but had deeper spiritual implications, indicating that the reason for keeping the commandments was for the spirit rather than the letter of the law. Another example is,

> *Ye have heard that it was said by them of old time, Thou shalt not commit adultery:*

> *But I say unto you, That whosoever looketh ...to lust ...hath committed adultery ...already in his heart.*   MATTHEW 5:27-28

Sheep were often used as a symbol of the children of God. Jesus told Peter to feed His sheep. He also said that He had other sheep that were not of His fold in Israel.

Older sheep are marked and help lead the flock.

Even clearer is the counsel,

> *Behold, I give unto you a commandment, that ye suffer [allow]*
> *none of these things to enter into your heart;   3 NEPHI 12:29*

The old and new laws are again like a chiasmus, with the Savior's ministry and subsequent atonement as the center, the turning point, linking the lesser and higher laws. The following poem illustrates the two principles.

Sermons on the Mounts

The law was given, the standard set. But, best was not accepted yet.
We compromised with Heaven's voice, just ten commandments was our choice.
Tooth for tooth and eye for eye, retribution was the cry.

Lesser Law

1. No other God -
2. Or image graven -
3. Not in vain, the name of Heaven -
4. Remember Sabbath,
5. Father, Mother -
6. Thou shalt not kill -
7. Nor defile another -
8. Do not steal -
9. Or false word belabor -
10. Do not covet the wealth of neighbor -

But then was promised a covenant new; inwardly, God would speak to you.
With sins forgiven and God revealed, a higher law on us was sealed.

Higher Law

10. Bless your neighbor -
9. Share a kindly word -
8. Give to others -
7. And clean thoughts preferred -
6. No need for anger to hide your smile -
5. Parents, children, walk the second mile -
4. Use the Sabbath, blessings to bestow -
3. The name of God in your good deeds show -
2. Your life will God's true image mirror,
1. As you and He become much nearer.

The secret of God's law is known—when action by intent is shown.
In Heaven's highest throne to stay, use thought and reason to guide the way.
The highest law is now defined—in thought, in spirit and in the mind.

— Daniel Rona

Chiasmus of the Law

The two sets of law form a chiasmus around the ministry and atonement of Jesus—the lesser law that would lead to him and the higher law to live like him. Fifty days after Jesus' crucifixion at Passover, the Holy Ghost came upon the congregation in Jerusalem. The Jewish holiday commemorating the giving of the lesser law at Mount Sinai is also celebrated fifty days after Passover. Apparently, the same day was also used in giving the gift of the Holy Ghost, the higher law. The day is called Pentecost.

> *And when the day of Pentecost was fully come, they were all with one accord in one place.*
>
> *And suddenly there came a sound from heaven as of a rushing mighty wind, and it filled all the house where they were sitting.*
>
> *And there appeared unto them cloven tongues like as of fire, and it sat upon each of them.*
>
> *And they were all filled with the Holy Ghost, and began to speak with other tongues, as the Spirit gave them utterance.*   ACTS 2:1-4

Sea of Galilee

Walking on the Water: Seven hundred feet below sea level the waters of the upper Jordan River feed and form the Sea of Galilee. Here, Jesus walked on the water; the Apostles were astonished and even frightened when they saw him.

> *But when they saw him walking upon the sea, they supposed it had been a spirit, and cried out... and were troubled...*   MARK 6:49-50

Jesus bid Peter to walk, but when Peter (rock) saw what danger he was in he began to sink. Peter cried out, "Save me." Jesus then helped him out of the water and said, "Wherefore didst thou doubt?" Was Jesus teaching Peter a very personal lesson? After all, Peter was crying out to be saved. Was Jesus reminding Peter that he did not need to doubt, that Jesus, the rock of salvation, came to save? Most of Jesus' miracles were very private and had great personal value for the recipients. We are privileged to also learn from them.

> *And in the fourth watch of the night Jesus went unto them, walking on the sea.*
>
> *And when the disciples saw him walking on the sea, they were troubled, saying, It is a spirit; and they cried out for fear.*
>
> *But straightway Jesus spake unto them, saying, Be of good cheer; it is I; be not afraid.*
>
> *And Peter answered him and said, Lord, if it be thou, bid me come unto thee on the water.*

Boats on The Sea of Galilee. The Sea of Galilee holds a wide variety of fish: sardines, catfish, mullets, carp, combfish, and one called St. Peter's fish. The Savior used a fish with a coin in its mouth from the Galilee to teach an important principle of generosity.

*And he said, Come. And when Peter was come down out of the
ship, he walked on the water, to go to Jesus.*

*But when he saw the wind boisterous, he was afraid; and
beginning to sink, he cried, saying, Lord, save me.*

*And immediately Jesus stretched forth his hand, and caught him,
and said unto him, O thou of little faith, wherefore didst thou doubt?*

*And when they were come into the ship, the wind ceased.
MATTHEW 14:25-32*

Sudden Storms on the Galilee: Due to the level of the lake (being about seven
hundred feet below sea level) and the heights of the surrounding hills (rising almost
ten thousand feet above sea level), sudden storms still arise on the Sea of Galilee.
Jesus calmed the wind and the waves, showing that he was the master of ocean and
earth and sky.   Some commented:

*...What manner of man is this, that even the wind and the sea
obey him? MARK 4:41 (see also 37-41)*

Catching Fish with Faith: Remember the sea story about Peter, who after fishing
all night without catching anything, was told to cast his nets on the other side of
the boat? He did and drew so many fish that the boat almost sank. Their nets broke,
and the fishermen were not able to draw the harvest.

*...Then he said unto Simon, Launch out into the deep, and let
down your nets for a draught.*

*And Simon answering said unto him, Master, we have toiled all
the night, and have taken nothing: nevertheless at thy word I will
let down the net.*

*And when they had this done, they inclosed a great multitude of
fishes: and their net brake.*

*And they beckoned unto their partners, which were in the other
ship, that they should come and help them. And they came, and
filled both the ships, so that they began to sink.   LUKE 5:4-7*

Fishers of Men: Jesus drew the fishermen away from their expertise and told them,

...I will make you fishers of men.   MATTHEW 4:19 (see also 18-20)

Another Chiasmus: It seems that a chiasmus was in the making. You see, after his
resurrection, the Savior appeared once more to the Apostles at the Sea of Galilee. Again,
they had been fishing all night—and had caught nothing. He told them,

...Cast the net on the right side of the ship,   JOHN 21:6 (see also 4-5)

*An Arab shepherd and his sheep
in the rolling hills of Israel. This
image was often used as a
model by the Savior to teach
his disciples about their
mission to teach the multitudes.*

The two stories of catching fish, one at the beginning of his earthly ministry and the second after his earthly ministry, point to the Savior's atonement as the center focus. The first time the disciples were told by Jesus to cast their nets on the other side, the nets broke; they were not able to harvest the fish. Three years later, he told them the second time to cast on the other side, this time the nets held together; and the disciples pulled in the catch. A symbolic consideration could be that their three years of training with the Master were to teach them to be worthy and capable as fishers of men.

Feed My Sheep: After the Resurrection, as the disciples successfully pulled the nets in, Jesus bade Peter and the others to eat with him. Jesus then asked Peter if he loved him more than the fishes. Three times Peter was led to say, "I love thee." Jesus then admonished him to "Feed my sheep."

> *So when they had dined, Jesus saith to Simon Peter, Simon, son of Jonas, lovest thou me more than these? He saith unto him, Yea, Lord; thou knowest that I love thee. He saith unto him, Feed my lambs.*
>
> *He saith to him again the second time, Simon, son of Jonas, lovest thou me? He saith unto him, Yea, Lord; thou knowest that I love thee. He saith unto him, Feed my sheep.*
>
> *He saith unto him the third time, Simon, son of Jonas, lovest thou me? Peter was grieved because he said unto him the third time, Lovest thou me? And he said unto him, Lord, thou knowest all things; thou knowest that I love thee. Jesus saith unto him, Feed my sheep.*   JOHN 21:15-17

Jesus' role is to save; the Apostles role is to feed the sheep. It seems that once the Twelve had learned that relationship, they were able to more successfully teach, effectively bless, and divinely save. They were then not doing things of themselves, but were truly working in the name of the Savior. There may be a very personal relationship in this significant dialogue with Peter who, just before the crucifixion, had denied knowing the Savior three times. Now, in an intimate moment he was given the opportunity to restate three times his love for his Master. Peter had "sunk to new heights."

Chapter 7

Galilee and South

Tiberias

A Roman Resort: The Roman resort town of Tiberias was started by Herod Antipas and still has hot sulfur springs used by many as a healing comfort.

Cemetery for Jewish Scholars: Tiberias later became a seat of Jewish learning and now contains the cemetery where some well-known Jewish scholars are buried. The great Jewish philosopher Maimonides is buried here. Almost eight hundred years ago, he wrote a *Guide to the Perplexed*, a work designed to bring Jews together in one Judaic belief. In that work are thirteen "Articles of Faith." The first three articles deal with the Judaic belief that God cannot be comprehended with human understanding.

Orthodox Christian God: It is interesting to note that the orthodox Christian concept of God is often expressed: "He is nowhere and yet everywhere, He fills the universe yet dwells in my heart." In that sense, the description of God by Jews and Christians is analogous—a God beyond human explanation and without anthropomorphic (manlike) characteristics.

Surveys of Christians and Jews indicate that people still want to imagine God in a father-like figure. Until eight centuries ago, Jewish sages and writers used anthropomorphic terms in describing God. Later we will examine the beliefs of other ancient Jews, the Essenes. They refer to God with manlike characteristics similar to those in the Old Testament, wherein references are made to God's face, hands, feet, and to his standing, speaking, and so forth.

"In the past decade, however, both Jews and Arabs have made the desert blossom as a rose."

The Jordan Valley

On the east side of the Jordan Valley was the ancient land of the tribes of Gad and Reuben.

Earthquake Rift: This below-sea-level Jordan Valley is an earthquake rift, the longest in the world. It extends from the Sea of Galilee in the north to Africa in the south.

The fault line is about four thousand miles long. Geologically, the rift divides two tectonic plates. The east plate moves slightly northward about 3/8 of an inch per year, and the west plate moves slightly southward about 3/8 of an inch per year. The total displacement is close to 3/4 of an inch per year and is a source of numerous minor and major tremors and earthquakes in the region. Evidences of past earthquakes are visible in the Essene communities' ruins at Qumran and at other archaeological excavations in the Jordan Valley.

Biblical Inhabitants of the Jordan: In biblical times, the patriarch Abraham gave his nephew, Lot, a choice of the lands he wanted to settle. Lot chose the eastern side of the Jordan Valley, the mountains of Moab. They had been green and fruitful at the time before Sodom and Gomorrah was destroyed.

> *And Lot lifted up his eyes, and beheld all the plain of Jordan, that it was well watered every where, before the Lord destroyed Sodom and Gomorrah, even as the garden of the Lord, like the land of Egypt, as thou comest unto Zoar.*

> *Then Lot chose him all the plain of Jordan; and Lot journeyed east: and they separated themselves the one from the other.*
> *GENESIS 13:10-11*

Later Moses assigned the tribes of Gad, Reuben, and part of Manasseh to inhabit the Jordan Valley.

> *And Moses gave unto them, even to the children of Gad, and to the children of Reuben, and unto half the tribe of Manasseh the son of Joseph, the kingdom of Sihon king of the Amorites, and the kingdom of Og king of Bashan, the land, with the cities thereof in the coasts, even the cities of the country round about.*
> *NUMBERS 32:33*

Now Blossoms as a Rose: Later this valley became a stark, desolate desert and has remained so for centuries. In the past decade, however, both Jews and Arabs have made the desert blossom as a rose.

> *The wilderness and the solitary place shall be glad for them; and the desert shall rejoice, and blossom as the rose.   ISAIAH 35:1*

With this in mind, it is certainly interesting to note that Israel exports more roses than does any other country in the world. The flower industry is the largest branch of Israel's agricultural economy. Flowers can be harvested, packaged, transported to the airport, flown to European markets, and marketed within twenty-four hours.

Desert Rains: Because of the agriculture introduced into this barren desert valley, the temperature has cooled. As the temperature has cooled, the clouds which used to drift eastward without letting their moisture loose have begun to precipitate. The annual recorded rainfall in some areas of the Jordan Valley has increased from about an inch (the identifying rating for a desert) to five and even six inches in recent years. Flash flooding has become a problem in the rainy season, too. Roadways are constantly being repaired during the winter months, as enormous amounts of rock and gravel grind their way down to the Dead Sea.

The "Living Waters" of the Jordan river
originating from the bedrock springs join
the muddy winter runoff of Mount Hermon.
In the lower Jordan River below the Sea of
Galilee, Jesus "The Fountain of Living
Waters" was baptized by immersion as an
example for all mankind. Orthodox Jews still
practice immersions today.

A Bedouin girl stands in the doorway of her father's tent near Jericho. There is a dramatic change of geological formations and weather as one travels from Jerusalem to Jericho. In the 15-mile drive up to Jerusalem the elevation changes 4,000 feet.

The Jordan River

Just south of Tiberias and at the lower part of the Sea of Galilee, the Jordan River continues its downward flow. It travels sixty-five miles to the Dead Sea but meanders two hundred miles to get there.

Baptisms at the Jordan: With the urging of the Israeli Ministry of Tourism, local residents have arranged a pleasant spot for Christians to be baptized here; but in the meridian of time, John, it seems, immersed Jesus in the Jordan River closer to Jericho, further down the Jordan Valley.

> *And he came into all the country about Jordan, preaching the baptism of repentance for the remission of sins... Now when all the people were baptized, it came to pass, that Jesus also being baptized, and praying, the heaven was opened, LUKE 3:3,21*

Baptism by Immersion: In the time of Jesus, as well as today, it was common for Jews to be immersed, often insisting that the water be "living water," that is, out of bedrock. It should also be flowing and always below ground level. Jesus' immersion was in the Jordan River which originates from bedrock springs—living water. The location described in the New Testament seems to be at the lowest spot on the face of the earth, below ground level of the rest of the world. The water flows into the Dead Sea. It seems symbolic, at least to me.

It is not surprising to suppose that Jesus was keeping a strict code of Mosaic tradition, immersion being part of that. Orthodox Jews still practice immersions quite regularly. It is from Jesus' example that Christians have adopted a baptismal practice; of course, some feel that baptism by immersion is still necessary, others perform baptism by a symbolic sprinkling.

The Dead Sea

Great Salt Lakes: The Jordan River flows into a lake called in Hebrew, "the Great Salt Lake." The term Dead Sea was given to it in later times. Its geographic and geological history is similar to America's Lake Bonneville in the Great Basin area of Utah. Later, that lake also became known as the Great Salt Lake. The reason for the Dead Sea's salt content is that many minerals flow into it and never flow out. It is estimated that up to seven million tons of water evaporate daily from the Dead Sea. The lake has no outlet. In ancient times it was enormous in size, but with evaporation and diminished flow into it, the Dead Sea became saturated with minerals. It is about as "thick" as water can be, about 27 percent mineral content.

Dead Sea Symbolism: There may be something symbolic about the disposition of this water body: always receiving and never giving. It is extremely unpleasant and bitter to the taste. That may happen with people who only receive—and never give—who are bitter, not "tasteful." An Apostle of Jesus used this metaphor when he taught,

> *I have shewed you all things, how that so labouring ye ought to support the weak, and to remember the words of the Lord Jesus, how he said, It is more blessed to give than to receive. ACTS 20:35*

The Desert

Israel's School: In the area southward from Galilee, one has descended into the Jordan Rift Desert. However, when one reaches the Dead Sea and then drives westward toward Jerusalem, a sudden change of geological formations, weather, as well as historical events, becomes obvious. It is interesting to note that ancient Israelites never tamed the desert completely. Instead, when they were sent to the wilderness, the desert was destined to tame them and to school them in the ways of their God. In his wisdom, God led the children of Israel into the desert where he could teach them to depend on him.

Prophets in the Desert: In Old Testament times, Isaiah prophetically announced that there would be a voice out of the wilderness to proclaim the Lord, who would lead the people out of bondage and through the wilderness.

> *The voice of him that crieth in the wilderness, Prepare ye the way
> of the Lord, make straight in the desert a highway for our God.*
> ISAIAH 40:3

John the Baptist raised his voice in announcing the coming of the Lord, Jesus.

> *He said, I am the voice of one crying in the wilderness, Make straight
> the way of the Lord, as said the prophet Esaias.*   JOHN 1:23

As the New Testament records, Jesus spent considerable time in the desert, fasting and being tempted. He provided an example of submission, yet great perseverance; of humility, and of great leadership.

Desert solitude.

Ship of the desert.

Chapter 8

Up to Jerusalem

Travelers to Jerusalem

 Up to Jerusalem: From the Dead Sea, an ancient highway goes up to Jerusalem. In just a dozen miles or so, there is a climb of about four thousand feet in elevation from thirteen hundred feet below sea level to about twenty-seven hundred feet above. The term "up to Jerusalem" has a physical as well as a spiritual implication. The ancient road out of Jericho leading to Jerusalem is rather desolate. Most of it is below sea level and below the rainfall line. It was, however, the road traveled by temple priests who lived in the Levite city of Jericho and served in Jerusalem's Temple. The travel was about a day's journey.

> *Then he took unto him the twelve, and said unto them, Behold, we go up to Jerusalem, and all things that are written by the prophets concerning the Son of man shall be accomplished.*   LUKE 18:31

Caravan Travel: Travelers in ancient times included animals in their caravans. The animals were used for transportation and food, as well as for barter. Travelers had to carry money for accommodations, so it was not wise to travel alone. As a support group and defense against highway robbers, caravans were organized and regularly scheduled.

Rules of Cleanliness: Special travel rules of cleanliness applied to the priests who had to remain "unblemished" to serve in the holy Temple. They stayed away from any decay or waste matter; and, of course, they kept at least a specific distance away from anything dead (unless it was killed as a sacrifice in the Temple).

> *And whosoever toucheth one that is slain with a sword in the open fields, or a dead body, or a bone of a man, or a grave, shall be unclean....*   NUMBERS 19:16

It is still a custom among some of those considering themselves to be Levites to circumvent graveyards or any place where there is death.

The Samaritan Inn: On the road from Jericho to Jerusalem, an old inn has been restored to represent the inn of a New Testament story Jesus told. Modern Christians refer to the inn as the "Good Samaritan Inn." The truth is that Jesus never used the term "Good Samaritan." The setting, however, can remind us of the parable Jesus chose as he answered a lawyer who challenged him, the Lawgiver:

> *...what shall I do to inherit eternal life?*   LUKE 10:25

"The city welcomes you with peace, Shalom in Hebrew, Salaam in Arabic, 'City of Shalom,' Jerusalem."

Jesus, the Master Craftsman

Carpenter or Craftsman: Information will be helpful in understanding why Jesus answered as he did. It is sometimes surprising to consider Jesus, known as *Rabbi*, to be a Master of the law (in Hebrew), instead of a carpenter. You'll remember, that the New Testament Greek word was not carpenter but craftsman. The craft in Nazareth was a huge stone quarry. It may be more than mere coincidence that Jesus was referred to as the "Rock of Salvation" and the "Chief Corner Stone." Was he sent to earth to be educated only as a craftsman or carpenter? Or is it more likely that Jesus studied the law that he was supposed to restore? After all, he is the lawgiver, our advocate with the Father.

> *...we have an advocate with the Father, Jesus Christ the righteous:*
> *1 JOHN 2:1*

Who is my Neighbor?

He was recognized as a rabbi, a lawyer, one schooled in the law; he was authorized to read in the synagogues.

> *And he came to Nazareth, where he had been brought up: and, as*
> *his custom was, he went into the synagogue on the sabbath day,*
> *and stood up for to read.*   *LUKE 4:16*

So, answering the lawyer who challenged Him and having been trained in the law himself, the new rabbi from Nazareth answered with a question,

> *What is written in the law? how readest thou?*   *LUKE 10:26*

Showing his own legal acumen, the lawyer recited the first law of loving God and neighbor, but challenged Jesus to a legal definition.

> *...who is my neighbour?*   *LUKE 10:29*

The Samaritan

The Parable: The Savior then related this story:

> *...A certain man went down from Jerusalem to Jericho, and fell*
> *among thieves, which stripped him of his raiment, and wounded*
> *him, and departed, leaving him half dead.*

> *And by chance there came down a certain priest that way: and*
> *when he saw him, he passed by on the other side.*

> *And likewise a Levite, when he was at the place, came and looked*
> *on him, and passed by on the other side.*

> *But a certain Samaritan [a non-Jew] ...came where he was:...*

An old inn on the road from Jericho to Jerusalem has been restored to represent the one mentioned by Jesus in His parable about the "Samaritan." This parable is a profound lesson in the difference between the letter and spirit of the Law.

> *...and bound up his wounds, pouring in oil and wine, and set him*
> *on his own beast, and brought him to an inn, and took care of him.*
> *LUKE 10:30-34*

Anti-Semitic Implications: Today local Jews don't use the term "Good" Samaritan; to some, it has anti-Semitic implications. I remember that an instructor of the Ministry of Tourism Guide Course even suggested that Jesus was an anti-Semite. She said, "Even when Jesus made up a story he portrayed the Jews as 'bad guys' and the non-Jew as the 'good guy.'"

Real Intent of Parable: Of course, Jesus had no intention of portraying Jews as uncompassionate. He was making a legal point in response to the lawyer's question, of legally, who is my neighbor? The Hebrew inference was that the priest and the Levite were within their legal rights—not to be defiled by being too close to the dead —and rather than take a chance, they went on the other side. Their lack of action was strictly legal, but it missed the higher law of compassion, governed by the spirit not the letter of the law. Talmudic commentary written some hundreds of years later indicates an additional guideline. Now Levites, or Cohens, are required to bury the dead if they chance upon a cadaver and are not accompanied by someone else.

Mount of Olives

Vineyards and Graves: Known for its biblically-renowned orchards and vineyards, this mount is also a sacred place for the dead. The Mount of Olives has been the hallowed resting spot for millennia of Jewish graves dating back almost three thousand years. The graves still point feet first toward the Temple Mount. It is a Jewish custom that all graves are directed feet first toward Jerusalem and in Jerusalem toward Temple Square. Recently, a gravestone with the name of King Uzziah inscribed on it was discovered on the Mount of Olives in the Russian Orthodox Church located adjacent to the graveyard. This was only discovered since 1967. It reads, "Hence were brought the bones of Uzziah the King—NOT TO BE OPENED!" The Bible indicates Uzziah's burial (about twenty-eight hundred years ago) was in the place where kings were buried, and that is most likely on the Mount of Olives.

> *Now the rest of the acts of Uzziah, first and last, did Isaiah the*
> *prophet, the son of Amoz, write.*
>
> *So Uzziah slept with his fathers, and they buried him with his*
> *fathers in the field of the burial which belonged to the kings...*
> *2 CHRONICLES 26:22-23*

Symbolic Stones on Graves: In a Jewish cemetery, you will notice small stones and rocks placed on the gravestones or monumental markers on or above the Jewish graves. This is a tradition indicating a yearning to have the Jerusalem Temple rebuilt. The temple functions contained sacred teachings of what was, what is, and what will be. Jews are also buried with a garment indicative of previous temple worship.

*Ancient triumphal city road on the
Mount of Olives.*

Samaritans still perform sacrifices.

Warning Signs for Jews and Levites

Do Not Touch the Dead: Approaching or leaving Jerusalem, one sees signs warning Jews who are Levites or consider themselves Cohens (as priests are called in Hebrew) not to travel further on this modern road, because it leads through a graveyard. As previously mentioned, ancient biblical tradition instructs a Levite or a Jewish priest not to touch anything dead—except for the unblemished firstborn sacrifice at the Temple. So rather than take a chance to be defiled by the emanations of the dead, even though they know the priesthood has been lost, modern Levites take another road on the other side of this Mount.

> *He that toucheth the dead body of any man shall be unclean....*
> *NUMBERS 19:11*

In modern times, there is an ultra-orthodox group which dedicates itself to the preservation and protection of the graves as well as to the protection from possible desecration of those who might pass by the grave sites. They put up the warning signs and station themselves on location of almost all the archaeological digs and construction projects, often creating a hindrance.

Jewish Temple Functions Ceased: Just as a reminder, Jews believe priestly temple functions ceased when the Temple was destroyed in 70 A.D. Many Jewish prayers end with the words, "...Jerusalem rebuilt." The rebuilding is a reference to the Temple they anticipate in the last days.

Jerusalem

Crown of Judean Hills: In coming "up to Jerusalem," the skyline of the city appears as a crown in the Judean Hills. It welcomes you with peace, Shalom! In our travels to Jerusalem we have considered archaeology, various historical accounts, traditions, and feelings. We have experienced the grandeur of the Golan, the peace of the Galilee, the rebirth of the desert, and the heavenly welcome of Jerusalem, the Holy City. From its modern name we can conclude that it is the place spoken of in the Bible,

> *In Salem also is his tabernacle, and his dwelling place in Zion.*
> *PSALM 76:2*

Yes, the city welcomes you with peace, *Shalom* in Hebrew, *Salaam* in Arabic, "City of Shalom," *Jerusalem*.

SCRIPTURAL REFERENCES (KJV)

Section Two

Features of Southern Israel

LEBANON

SYRIA

Caesarea
Philippi

Golan

Capernaum

Haifa Cana Sea of
Galilee
Tiberias

Nazareth

Armageddon

Caesarea

Giladi

Mediterranean Sea

Jordan River

Tel Aviv
Jaffa

Jericho

Qumran

Jerusalem
Bethlehem Bethany

Bet Shemesh

Dead Sea

JORDAN

Elah

Hebron

Beersheva Masada

EGYPT

Elat

- Overview -
The living desert

A road from **JERUSALEM** to **JERICHO** is the desolate setting for the **"GOOD" SAMARITAN** story described in the previous chapter. As you descend from Jerusalem, **JERICHO** greets you with a refreshing oasis. It is the oldest walled city in the world. Close by is the **DEAD SEA**, the lowest place on the face of the earth. At **QUMRAN** you will see the caves where the Dead Sea Scrolls were found. The high point of this section is **MASADA**, an amazing mountaintop fortress built by Herod and later taken over by Jewish Zealots. Masada is accessible by a four-minute cable-car ride rising nearly fifteen hundred feet. The story of the Zealots' last stand is dramatically visualized at these impressive ruins. Further south is **BEERSHEVA**, a modern city with **BEDOUIN** who still keep ancient customs. **EILAT**, the port on the **RED SEA**, has one of the world's finest coral reserves. Returning northward to the **HILLS OF JUDEA**, you see **HEBRON**, one of the oldest cities in civilization. Close by is where **DAVID** and **GOLIATH** battled in the **VALLEY OF ELAH**. Along the foothills, the **SHEPHELAH**, a few miles northward is **BET SHEMESH**, where **SAMSON** had his affairs. The corridor up to Jerusalem is known as the famous **BAB EL WAD**, the main road to Jerusalem.

*An ancient Essene community lived at Qumran.
Their religious writings were written on scrolls,
placed in clay jars, and hidden in these caves.
They were not seen again for 2,000 years
until they were found accidentally by
some Bedouin shepherd boys.*

Chapter 9

Jerusalem to The Dead Sea

Jerusalem

 Name of Jerusalem: No other city has been mentioned as much in the Bible as Jerusalem. Somehow other modern cities' traditions pale against the over four-thousand-year history of this holy city. Jerusalem was once a Jebusite city before David conquered it. It probably gets its modern name from the title of Salem. *Salem* is the word "peace," *Salaam* in Arabic, *Shalom* in Hebrew. It is also known by other names, such as Zion, Ariel, Al Quds, City of the Lord, or simply, the Holy City. Just the mention of Jerusalem invokes the thought of looking up to the "mountain of the Lord's house." From any direction, Jerusalem can only be reached by coming "up" to Mount Moriah, where the ancient Jerusalem Temple stood.

> *In Salem also is his tabernacle, and his dwelling place in Zion.*
> PSALM 76:2

> *And it shall come to pass in the last days, that the mountain of the Lord's house shall be established in the top of the mountains, and shall be exalted above the hills; and all nations shall flow unto it.*
> ISAIAH 2:2

Holy Site for Many Faiths: Jerusalem is the focal point for the most important religious events of Judaism and Christianity. For the Jews, Jerusalem is the location of the Lord's house. For Latter-day Saints, Salt Lake City is the location for the Lord's house. Both are correct; the prophecy is a parallel, a reference to two Zions. Jerusalem has become the third most holy site for Islam. The Savior's greatest gift to humanity came and will come from Jerusalem. We'll examine these events in detail as the history and sites of the city are described. Today the city spreads over a cluster of seven hills and has six principal canyons leading up to it. Each canyon ends by a hill or mount that overlooks the city of Jerusalem. Presently, as in the past, each hill acts as a populated guardian or fortress for the city. In that sense, the city is surrounded by a "wall of people."

My Home in Gilo: I live in Jerusalem on the hill named Gilo, a mile north of Bethlehem. It is probably the same town of Giloh in King David's time.

> *And Absalom sent for Ahithophel the Gilonite, David's counsellor, from his city, even from Giloh, while he offered sacrifices. And the conspiracy was strong; for the people increased continually with Absalom.* 2 SAMUEL 15:12

"A part of every ancient book of the Old Testament except the book of Esther was found in these writings, including the entire book of Isaiah."

*An Arab family works in the field as their
sheep feed on the rock terraces near
Jericho and the Dead Sea.*

The Arabic name for Giloh is "Jala," and the modern day village of Bet Jala is just a mile from Bethlehem, a little south of the Jewish residences of Gilo. The name connection is still there, even though the spelling may differ in various languages.

Jerusalem Is Like a Hand: Jerusalem is spread out much like the palm of your right hand—facing up. The roads in and out of Jerusalem are like your fingers and wrist. The "thumb" points north and leads to Samaria. The "pointer finger" points northwest and leads towards Modiin where Judas the Macabee lived (He started the Jewish holiday of Hanukkah). The "middle finger" points westward and leads to Bet Shemesh where Samson had his affairs. The "ring finger" points southwestern and leads to the Valley of Elah where David made such an impression on Goliath! The "little or pinky finger" points southward and leads to Bethlehem where sheep and shepherds still reside. The "wrist to the elbow" approach points eastward and leads to Jericho where the walls came tumbling down.

Jerusalem to Jericho and the Dead Sea

A Contrast of Scenery: The area from Jerusalem to the Dead Sea is a contrast like no other. The annual rainfall in the Judean Hills is the same as in London (about twenty-three to twenty-six inches per year), but just about a dozen miles away, the Jordan Desert and the Dead Sea receive but a few drops (historically, less than one inch per year). Here the lower Jordan River empties into the Dead Sea. The area around the Dead Sea has looked much like a moonscape, but the greenery from the tops of the Judean Hills is now being brought to the desert. As you see the contrasts of desert and fruitful green fields, you may well wonder what God had in mind to have led the ancient covenant people of Israel from Moab and across the Jordan River to this harsh desert area.

> *...the people removed from their tents, to pass over Jordan,...and the people passed over right against Jericho....and all the Israelites passed over on dry ground, until all the people were passed clean over Jordan.* JOSHUA 3:14, 16-17

The Walls of Jericho: Just north of the Dead Sea, you find Jericho nestled at the bottom of the Judean Hills. You can still discover a quiet town of fruit and vegetable growers. It is a trade-route city that has encountered at least twenty-eight different conquests, as evidenced in the excavations of this ancient tel. One of those conquests was by Joshua, who led the Israelites on six silent daily walks around the walls of the city. On the seventh day they made another six silent walks around the city. All the noiseless marching may have confused the ancient inhabitants of Jericho. It was the seventh walk around the city on the seventh day that was made noisily. Accompanied by trumpets and shouts, the walls came tumbling down!

> *And the Lord said unto Joshua, See, I have given into thine hand Jericho...*
>
> *And ye shall compass the city, all ye men of war, and go round about the city once. Thus shalt thou do six days.*

And it came to pass on the seventh day, that they rose early about the dawning of the day, and compassed the city after the same manner seven times: only on that day they compassed the city seven times.

And it came to pass at the seventh time, when the priests blew with the trumpets, Joshua said unto the people, Shout; for the Lord hath given you the city.   JOSHUA 6:2-3, 15-16

Achan Stoned for Coveting Wealth: During the conquest of Jericho, the prophet Joshua commanded that all living persons and animals were to be killed except for Rahab (the harlot who had saved the Israelite spies). All gold, silver and other metal, and worthwhile items were to be brought to the Lord's treasury. Though no loot was to be taken at Jericho, a certain man named Achan succumbed to the temptation of wealth and took some spoils. Because he took a Babylonish garment, two hundred shekels of silver, and a wedge of gold and hid them in his tent, the Israelites experienced a terrible defeat at their next battle. After Joshua individually interviewed each man, he found Achan, who confessed the theft. He and his entire family were stoned to death and then, with all of their possessions, they were burned with fire.

And Achan answered Joshua, and said, Indeed I have sinned against the Lord God of Israel, and thus and thus have I done:

When I saw among the spoils a goodly Babylonish garment, and two hundred shekels of silver, and a wedge of gold of fifty shekels weight, then I coveted them, and took them; and, behold, they are hid in the earth in the midst of my tent, and the silver under it.

So Joshua sent messengers, and they ran unto the tent; and, behold, it was hid in his tent, and the silver under it.

And they took them out of the midst of the tent, and brought them unto Joshua, and unto all the children of Israel, and laid them out before the Lord.

...And Joshua said, Why hast thou troubled us? the Lord shall trouble thee this day. And all Israel stoned him with stones, and burned them with fire, after they had stoned them with stones. JOSHUA 7:20, 23-25

Mount of Temptation: As recorded in the New Testament, Jesus was tempted with the wealth of the world by Satan. This probably happened at Jericho, an oasis, and an important and busy crossroads. This way station was obviously a place of wealth, natural and manmade. The Mount of Temptation just above Jericho marks the traditional spot where Jesus' temptation may have occurred.

Again, the devil taketh him up into an exceeding high mountain, and sheweth him all the kingdoms of the world, and the glory of them;

Near the city of Jericho is the traditional
Mount of Temptation where Jesus was
tempted with wealth by Satan. There is a
monastery on the Mount.

And saith unto him, All these things will I give thee, if thou wilt fall down and worship me.

Then saith Jesus unto him, Get thee hence, Satan: for it is written, Thou shalt worship the Lord thy God, and him only shalt thou serve.   MATTHEW 4:8-10

A monastery has been built into the side of the mount. Tradition indicates that for many years the monastery was "wordless." Possibly this was done in symbolic gesture of the silent walks the Israelites made around the site.

Tax Collector in a Tree: When Jesus was teaching at Jericho, the tax collector, Zacchaeus, climbed a tree to better see him. Jesus invited himself to Zacchaeus's house to dine with him. People murmured that Jesus was socializing with the expropriator of their taxes. It is interesting to note that tax collectors had to reach a quota set by the Romans. It was imperative that taxes were collected above the normal rate when the economy was good so that the quota could be met when the economy was bad. The people murmured that Zacchaeus may have abused that system for his own benefit. However, a better look into his personality shows differently, or at least indicates a complete change. Zacchaeus was so impressed with Jesus' teachings that he offered half of his wealth to the poor and fourfold repayment to the people he had wronged.

And Jesus entered and passed through Jericho.

And, behold, there was a man named Zacchaeus, which was the chief among the publicans, and he was rich.

And he sought to see Jesus who he was; and could not for the press, because he was little of stature.

And he ran before, and climbed up into a sycomore tree to see him: for he was to pass that way.

And when Jesus came to the place, he looked up, and saw him, and said unto him, Zacchaeus, make haste, and come down; for to day I must abide at thy house.

And he made haste, and came down, and received him joyfully.

And when they saw it, they all murmured, saying, That he was gone to be guest with a man that is a sinner.

And Zacchaeus stood, and said unto the Lord; Behold, Lord, the half of my goods I give to the poor; and if I have taken any thing from any man by false accusation, I restore him fourfold.   LUKE 19:1-8

Old displaced persons' homes in Jericho reflect the style and structure of ancient houses in Israel. They are made of stone and clay with a flat roof. During the hottest time of the year, families often sleep on the roof of this type of house.

A tree in Jericho marks the traditional site of that event. I recall that some professional tree surgeons touring with me a few years ago remarked that the supposed Zacchaeus tree looked more like two hundred years old than two thousand. Fortunately, it's not the tree but the story that is important.

The three Jericho stories have some connection to wealth. Achan succumbed to temptation, disobeyed, and stole. Jesus was tempted, but refused the wealth of the world. And Zacchaeus was willing to repay his wrongs even fourfold.

Everything Belongs to God: The important lesson underlying these accounts is that there is no ownership; it is all stewardship. Everything belongs to the Lord. Whatever wealth man assembles is a test of his stewardship.

Qumran

In the same period of history, another community was situated close by the Dead Sea, sharing what little wealth they had in a common unity. The ruins of Qumran echo the history of a people supposed by many to be the Essenes.

The Dead Sea Scrolls: The Dead Sea Scrolls were found quite by accident by some Bedouin boys. Apparently they were throwing stones into cavities of rock as they explored one of the many holes and caves by the Dead Sea. They entered one cave where one of their stones had struck a clay jar which had lain hidden for close to two thousand years. Wrapped in musty cloth, the leather scrolls in the clay jars were meaningless to them, but eventually they pawned them off for a "few dollars" to a shoemaker in Bethlehem. He was able to sell them for a substantial sum to a Jewish scholar, Dr. Eliezar Sukenik, who recognized their immense historical and religious value.

After the scrolls were discovered, the Bedouin began combing the caves for more inventory to sell. In one case, they began to cut leather scrolls into strips so they had more inventory. The French and Jordanians secured the area to protect the antiquities.

Essene Community: The nearby ruins have now become significant and are being excavated. Living quarters, writing halls, cisterns, and immersion fonts indicate a religious Jewish life of two thousand years ago. It is not strange to find immersion fonts in this community; after all, Jews still practice immersions today. Many religious Jews feel that water used in ritual immersions must be spring water, or "living water." Nearby are numerous springs as well as the Jordan River which is fed by springs from the northern Galilee. The scriptures indicate that John the Baptist was immersing in the Jordan River; very possibly it was at a point close by. Mormons and others are comfortable with the term "baptism." The Jews, however, see baptism as a renunciation of being a Jew (a perceived kind of anti-Semitism). So we'll continue to use the term immersion. Incidentally, conversion to Judaism requires, among other things, a complete immersion.

Contents of Scrolls: A part of every ancient book of the Old Testament except the book of Esther was found in these writings, including the entire book of Isaiah.

Oldest Biblical Writings: These biblical writings are a thousand years older than any previously known Hebrew biblical text. Some Qumran biblical books have additional written texts other than the ones we know today. There are references to other writings that are now lost to us. The Essenes also wrote prolifically about their own interpretations and plans for the near future. They seemed to consider that they were in the "latter days" and even planned to rebuild the existing temple

A view from inside one of the caves at Qumran where clay jars containing ancient leather scrolls were found in 1947. The scrolls are now regarded as the most important archaeological find of the twentieth century.

in Jerusalem. The best-preserved parts of these scrolls are displayed at the Israel Museum in Jerusalem at the Shrine of the Book. We'll learn more about the Dead Sea Scrolls in another chapter.

Ein Gedi

An Oasis at the Dead Sea: The most outstanding display of nature and scenery at the Dead Sea is undoubtedly the oasis of Ein Gedi.

> *My beloved is unto me as a cluster of camphire in the vineyards of En-gedi.   SONG OF SOLOMON 1:14*

Cold fresh water as well as hot sulfur springs still flow out of the Judean mountains.

Kibbutz Ein Gedi: The Kibbutz Ein Gedi is known for its remarkable farming; it also has a youth hostel and cafeteria and boasts of naturally hot and cold running water. The natural hot springs and fresh waterfalls are an attraction enjoyed by many tourists and a constant draw for Israelis who particularly enjoy hiking. The Kibbutz Ein Gedi operates a successful spa which attracts visitors from all over the world who take advantage of the healing properties of the Dead Sea. The spa as well as hotels in the area have resident nurses and medical practitioners to assist visitors in their specialized therapies for treating arthritic conditions, psoriasis, eczema and other skin difficulties. The famous Hadassah Medical Organization encourages doctors to use the healing effects of the Dead Sea. Health-care programs around the world have begun to recognize the dramatic healing effect these unusual waters provide. There are numerous sulphur and fresh-water springs that come out of the mountains and flow into the Dead Sea.

King Saul and David: Two thousand years ago, Jewish Zealots retreated to nearby caves in order to hide from the Romans who were not used to mountain climbing and cave searches. A thousand years before that, David, escaping the murderous intent of Saul, hid in nearby caves. Saul, searching for David, went into a cave

> *...to cover his feet...   1 SAMUEL 24:3*

(a scriptural way of saying he went to relieve himself). David was in that same cave. He cut off a part of Saul's cloak but would not kill him. As Saul left, David showed himself and said,

> *...I will not put forth mine hand against my lord; for he is the Lord's anointed.   1 SAMUEL 24:10*

Saul then replied,

> *And now, behold, I know well that thou shalt surely be king, and that the kingdom of Israel shall be established in thine hand. 1 SAMUEL 24:20*

When David refused to kill the "Lord's anointed," he was symbolically teaching that Saul, too, should not be trying to kill the anointed king. (Remember, David had already been anointed to be the king of Israel.)

The Dead Sea has a 27% mineral content.
Much like the Great Salt Lake in Utah, it is
possible for a person to float easily in the
water. At 1,300 feet below sea level, this is
also the lowest place on the face of the Earth.

The Dead Sea

Mineral Content: The mineral content of the Dead Sea is about 27 percent. That is the maximum mineral saturation water can have at this elevation and temperature. A mineral extraction plant is located on its southern shore at Sdom; the name is probably derived from the ancient name Sodom. Minerals and derivatives are exported throughout the world. Minerals included in the unusual body of water are magnesium, bromides, calcium chloride, and sodium chloride. Potash is also derived from the Dead Sea. Common table salt originates here as well. The Dead Sea is the world's largest concentration of what is commonly called liquid metal or magnesium. The potash mined from the lake is easily stored below sea level. Anywhere else the potash liquifies, but below sea level it stays in its powdery state. This makes an important impact on its marketability. The low elevation is also one of the reasons why the Dead Sea Scrolls were preserved so well.

Lot's Wife and Salt: As the water evaporates from the lake, the high concentration of salt and minerals crystallize and form "pillars." I suppose one of them could be called "Lot's Wife"—the pillar of the community! This is probably the area she lived in when she was "turned to salt."

> Then the Lord rained upon Sodom and upon Gomorrah brimstone and fire from the Lord out of heaven;
>
> And he overthrew those cities, and all the plain, and all the inhabitants of the cities, and that which grew upon the ground.
>
> But his wife looked back from behind him, and she became a pillar of salt.   GENESIS 19:24-26

Lowest Place on Earth: At thirteen hundred feet below sea level, the Dead Sea is the lowest place on the face of the earth. It is also thirteen hundred feet deep. The lake's level has been hundreds of feet higher in ancient times, but today it is receding rapidly. Sir William Matthew Flinders Petrie, a British Egyptologist and archaeologist, made a measurement mark of the Dead Sea more than eighty years ago. The lake's level has dropped close to eighty feet in eighty years.

The Great Salt Lake: As mentioned in the previous section, nothing lives in it. Yet in Hebrew it is not referred to generally as the Dead Sea, but more often as the Great Salt Lake. (The words "lake," "sea," and even "ocean" are simply *yam* in Hebrew.)

> All these were joined together in the vale of Siddim, which is the salt sea.   GENESIS 14:3
>
> And the border shall go down to Jordan, and the goings out of it shall be at the salt sea: this shall be your land with the coasts thereof round about.   NUMBERS 34:12
>
> And the east border was the salt sea, even unto the end of Jordan. And their border in the north quarter was from the bay of the sea at the uttermost part of Jordan: JOSHUA 15:5

Chapter 10

Masada to Eilat

Masada

Herod's Fortress: Herod the Great chose the lifeless surroundings of this area to build two palaces on a naturally separated mesa. Built fifteen hundred feet above the Dead Sea, totally isolated and without life support, Masada became an ancient Palm Springs. It was also a fortress to protect Herod from his real or imagined enemies. Magnificent buildings, pools, baths, and fountains defied nature. There were enormous food-storage chambers and many plastered cisterns carefully surrounded by double walls and lookout towers. After Herod's death, Roman soldiers continued to use this pleasure palace but later were unexpectedly routed by Jewish Zealots who climbed undetected into this remote Roman garrison.

The Siege of Masada: Later, in planning to retake the fortress, the Romans set up a siege of the mountain. This was more difficult for the Romans below than for the Jews above who had supplies and stored water. The Romans started to fill in the canyon on the western side of the mount and to build a ramp to the top. Josephus, a Jewish-turned-Roman historian, tells us that the Jews stopped the Romans from building the ramp by throwing boulders down on them. The Romans then brought in Jewish slaves from Jerusalem, which had just been destroyed, to build the ramp, thereby keeping the Jews at the top from hurdling rock and stopping the work on the ramp. In the end, more than 960 men, women, and children collectively decided to end their own lives, choosing death rather than surrender to the Romans.

Masada Scriptures and Life After Death: Excavations made between 1963 and 1967 confirmed many of these strange, almost unbelievable facts which Josephus had written about some nineteen hundred years ago. Archaeologists found that the Zealots apparently constructed a synagogue. It is considered the oldest synagogue built since the Herodian Temple was destroyed in Jerusalem. It had an entrance leading to Jerusalem. The innermost part of this three-courtyard worship center was in the *geniza*, a storage room for Torah scrolls. Only fragments of scriptures were found. The largest of these fragments was the thirty-seventh chapter of Ezekiel.

What makes this unique is that the Zealots' credo was, "Death rather than slavery." The chapter discovered deals with life after death.

> *The hand of the Lord was upon me, and carried me out in the spirit of the Lord, and set me down in the midst of the valley which was full of bones,*

"The Ezekiel chapter of 'coming alive again' is found among the ruins of those who collectively held to the concept of dying rather than living a life in slavery."

*Masada was built by Herod the Great as a
winter palace and fortress. It was taken over by
Jewish Zealots. In A.D. 73, after a lengthy siege.
The Roman army finally entered Masada only to
find that the inhabitants had all died at their
own hands rather than live under Roman rule.*

And caused me to pass by them round about: and, behold, there were very many in the open valley; and, lo, they were very dry. And he said unto me, Son of man, can these bones live? And I answered, O Lord GOD, thou knowest.

Again he said unto me, Prophesy upon these bones, and say unto them, O ye dry bones, hear the word of the Lord.

Thus saith the Lord GOD unto these bones; Behold, I will cause breath to enter into you, and ye shall live:

And I will lay sinews upon you, and will bring up flesh upon you, and cover you with skin, and put breath in you, and ye shall live; and ye shall know that I am the Lord.

So I prophesied as I was commanded: and as I prophesied, there was a noise, and behold a shaking, and the bones came together, bone to his bone.

And when I beheld, lo, the sinews and the flesh came up upon them, and the skin covered them above: but there was no breath in them.

Then said he unto me, Prophesy unto the wind, prophesy, son of man, and say to the wind, Thus saith the Lord GOD; Come from the four winds, O breath, and breathe upon these slain, that they may live.

So I prophesied as he commanded me, and the breath came into them, and they lived, and stood up upon their feet, an exceeding great army.   EZEKIEL 37:1-10

The Resurrection: There is more symbolism to be seen in this chapter as the ancient prophet continues to compare the once-dead bones that come alive in the Resurrection with the restoration of the entire house of Israel. It is a resurrection of the once-dead nation of Israel.

Then he said unto me, Son of man, these bones are the whole house of Israel: behold, they say, Our bones are dried, and our hope is lost: we are cut off for our parts.

Therefore prophesy and say unto them, Thus saith the Lord GOD; Behold, O my people, I will open your graves, and cause you to come up out of your graves, and bring you into the land of Israel.

And ye shall know that I am the Lord, when I have opened your graves, O my people, and brought you up out of your graves,

And shall put my spirit in you, and ye shall live, and I shall place you in your own land: then shall ye know that I the Lord have spoken it, and performed it, saith the Lord.   EZEKIEL 37:11-14

Two Sticks to Become One: The verses that follow contain even more information that is linked with coming alive again. It seems like a play on the root words for "sticks" and "bones." On one hand, the word for "bones" is *etzemot*, and on the other hand the word for "sticks" is *etz*. If etz is considered the root, then one could assume etzemot as a plural form for etz. The bones or skeleton of a once true and living religion is the "stick of Judah," the Bible. The flesh on the bones could be likened to the "stick of Joseph," the Book of Mormon. When God blew the breath of life into the combining of the two sticks, the one true and living religion came alive again. The one true principle of resurrection came alive again as well.

> *The word of the Lord came again unto me, saying,*
>
> *Moreover, thou son of man, take thee one stick, and write upon it, For Judah, and for the children of Israel his companions: then take another stick, and write upon it, For Joseph, the stick of Ephraim, and for all the house of Israel his companions:*
>
> *And join them one to another into one stick; and they shall become one in thine hand.*
>
> *And when the children of thy people shall speak unto thee, saying, Wilt thou not shew us what thou meanest by these?*
>
> *Say unto them, Thus saith the Lord GOD; Behold, I will take the stick of Joseph, which is in the hand of Ephraim, and the tribes of Israel his fellows, and will put them with him, even with the stick of Judah, and make them one stick, and they shall be one in mine hand.*
>
> *And the sticks whereon thou writest shall be in thine hand before their eyes.*   EZEKIEL 37:15-20

Mormons and Masada: Latter-day Saints feel that the Bible prophecy found at Masada referring to the two sticks (families) connects their scriptures (Bible and the Book of Mormon) to the families of the tribes of Judah and Joseph. There is no other historical connection of Mormons and Masada. What is interesting is that the Ezekiel chapter of "coming alive again" is found among the ruins of those who collectively held to the concept of dying rather than living a life in slavery.

The Real Spirit of Masada: The spirit of collective identity is still felt strongly here as Israeli children and soldiers visit Masada at least once in their military or educational pursuits. Some young Jewish lads come here for their Bar Mitzvahs. In the past, elite Israeli military forces took their oaths at this ancient fortress with the cry, "Masada shall never fall again!"

Although the honor and memory of the Zealots' resolve is maintained, the young Israeli today has some doubts as to the necessity of their actions. It is said that the underlying reason to take Masada from the Roman garrison was senseless, since there was no military or strategic significance for the fortress. It served only for the recreation and pleasure of the Roman soldiers. Its conquest did not serve the Zealots, nor for that matter, the Romans who subsequently retook it. In that sense, the battle of Masada was a battle of spite. Many young military people, who are

*Donkeys have carried the burdens of Israel
for thousands of years. It was a small
donkey that carried the Savior during
His triumphal entry into Jerusalem just
one week before He was crucified.*

There are almost two million Arabs and Bedouin in Israel. Some still live nomadic lifestyles in the desert. Their way of life is much the same as the ancient Israelites more than two thousand years ago.

serving their country today, feel that the Zealots nineteen hundred years ago were misdirected. To them, the taking of Masada was inconsequential and Zealot lives were lost for an unjustified reason. The memories of Masada faded as the ruins crumbled and were picked over by nomadic Bedouin traversing this desert area during the last two thousand years.

Arabs and Bedouin

Children of the Desert: Today some of the Arabs (descendants of Ishmael) and also the Bedouin (probably descendants of Keturah, one of the wives of Abraham) still live nomadic lives, wandering the wilderness area, oasis to oasis. Their lifestyle differs little from that of their ancestors who lived thousands of years ago. Tents are still made of goat hair strands woven together, and the tents are still aligned in a north-south direction with the tent openings to the east. There are special customs for visiting that guests should understand and follow.

How to Visit a Bedouin: Visitors ought to approach from the west and the north, coming to the clan leader or *sheikh* who will invite them to his tent. Bitter coffee is then served and lengthy conversations are carried out, followed by a serving of sweet tea. Once a guest is accepted (having progressed from the "bitter to the sweet"), more coffee beans are baked and rhythmically crushed in a special pot (usually a hand-carved family heirloom). The rhythmical grinding of the coffee is a sign to the rest of the clan that an extra guest will stay for dinner. Meals are prepared in a one-pot style, served heaping on a tray, and placed in the middle of the tent. Guests and family are seated around the tray. Food is to be eaten only with the right hand. Guests are always expected to eat first, the men eat next, and women and children eat last.

Today's Bedouin Lifestyle: To the Bedouin, time may seem to have stood still, although evidences of the twentieth century can be seen with television sets (often battery operated) and motor vehicles parked by their tents (prominently placed for all to see). Most of the Bedouin live in the Negev, around Beersheva. Their lifestyle is changing from tribal north-south tent dwelling to modern north-south stone and cement houses. They are becoming organized, electing their own town officials and putting their representatives in national government. They are pleased that their own Bedouin people now are administrating their school system, as well as the advanced agricultural facilities that the State of Israel has helped them establish.

A Visit to Sheikh Abu Taha: On one visit to a Bedouin sheikh named Abu Taha, it was apparent that he was interested in pleasing us and showing off his fading culture. He had prepared the coffee beans for grinding, and a fire was smoldering in his tent. We approached from the north and west and waited until he motioned us in. I had sent a message ahead that many on the tour were not coffee drinkers, so he graciously sent one of his children (he had over twenty from four wives) to fetch soft drinks for us. Timelessly, he proceeded with the ritual of grinding and baking the beans and then serving the coffee.

Modern Ideas from the Sheikh's Son: One of his children, a handsome looking twenty-year old, translated his father's Arabic into correct English and Hebrew. The young man politely scolded some for not drinking the traditional coffee. Later he confided in us that he didn't drink coffee either. He was a student of botany and plant physiology at the nearby Ben Gurion University. The sheikh's son had adopted a health code that was different from his family's custom; however, he still taught us the old traditions anyway. The sheikh was pleased with his son's modern thinking and gave his son the only automobile the family owned. Camels were tethered outside, still being used for everyone else's transportation.

Much of the Negev Desert has been reserved for Bedouin living; they transport agricultural goods into nearby cities. Although their culture is being westernized, the contrast of their desert lifestyle to the standard of twentieth-century living is still dramatic.

The Negev

Blossoms Like a Rose: Since the State of Israel was established in 1948, David Ben-Gurion's dream of making the desert blossom like a rose has been fulfilled in many ways. Ben Gurion was Israel's first Prime Minister. The Negev has been an important trade route for thousands of years. It was the inheritance of the tribe of Simeon.

> *And the second lot came forth to Simeon, even for the tribe of the children of Simeon according to their families: and their inheritance was within the inheritance of the children of Judah.*
>
> *And they had in their inheritance Beer-sheba, or Sheba, and Moladah. JOSHUA 19:1-2*

Ancient Cisterns: In modern times, those settling the Negev Desert, digging for water and excavating ruins, have found ancient channels and cisterns that were used for water collection. Anciently, Abraham settled parts of this desert by digging wells.

> *For all the wells which his father's servants had digged in the days of Abraham his father, the Philistines had stopped them, and filled them with earth. GENESIS 26:15 (see also 18)*

Beersheva

Home of Abraham: Beersheva was also the home of Abraham. Here, Hagar, a wife of Abraham, was blessed by an angel as she left Abraham's tent and traveled with her son, Ishmael.

> *...and the angel of God called to Hagar out of heaven, and said unto her, What aileth thee, Hagar? fear not; for God hath heard the voice of the lad where he is.*
>
> *Arise, lift up the lad, and hold him in thine hand; for I will make him a great nation. GENESIS 21:17-18*

An Arab woman waits for a bus under a tree in Beersheva. This ancient village was one of Abraham's homes. He planted a grove of trees here. The name Beersheva means "seven wells," making this a fruitful area.

Meaning of Beersheva: The name Beersheva means "seven wells." It also means a "well of the oath," probably referring to the oath Abraham made with the anointed king of Gerar, which is close by. The wells of Beersheva indicate that there was plenty of ground water; so in spite of being in the Negev Desert, Beersheva became known for its rich pasture lands.

> *And Abraham planted a grove in Beer-sheba, and called there on the name of the Lord, the everlasting God.* GENESIS 21:33

The Southern Border of Israel: In ancient times it marked the southern border of Israel.

> *Then all the children of Israel went out, and the congregation was gathered together as one man, from Dan even to Beer-sheba, with the land of Gilead, unto the Lord in Mizpeh.* JUDGES 20:1

Archaeological Excavations: The ancient tel (archaeological site) of Beersheva has been excavated and partially restored. In the excavations, parts of a religious altar and ruins of the ancient wall were found in the debris. These pieces have been reassembled and give us a good idea of the size and shape of ancient altars. A scriptural reference seems to indicate that "high places" (worship centers with altars) were destroyed from "Geba to Beersheva." It can be assumed that the broken altar pieces were buried or used in the construction of the wall of the city.

> *And he brought all the priests out of the cities of Judah, and defiled the high places where the priests had burned incense, from Geba to Beer-sheba, and brake down the high places of the gates that were in the entering in of the gate of Joshua the governor of the city, which were on a man's left hand at the gate of the city.* 2 KINGS 23:8

Industry and Agriculture: In modern times, Beersheva has become a thriving center for industry and agriculture. From just three hundred people in 1948, Beersheva has grown to over one hundred sixty thousand inhabitants who have developed a flourishing infrastructure that supports an internationally recognized university. There are worldwide business ventures such as ceramic, chemical, and mineral production centered in this ancient/modern city.

Eilat

City with a View: South of the Negev and at the northern tip of the Sinai is a tropical sea. With its breathtaking view, the modern city of Eilat grows into the barren, rugged Sinai mountains that surround a blue mirror-like gulf called the Red Sea. Settled in the 1960s, Eilat has become a successful commercial seaport, connecting Israeli markets with the Suez Canal in Egypt. A population of about 20 thousand entertains and services more than ten times that many tourists. Sun seekers from Europe and Scandinavia flock to the warm tropical waters. Regular charter flights bring thousands yearning for Eilat's sunshine and crystal clear waters.

Underwater Wonders: The underwater coral and sea life provide remarkable grandeur for such a small area and attract hundreds of thousands of visitors every year. Describing the splendor, a world-renowned audiophile, David Wilson, once said: "The view underwater to my eyes is what stereo is to my ears." The surprising difference of Eilat is part of the gift of Israel. Israel—the grandeur of her sites, the diversity of her history, but most of all the warmth of her spirit, a spirit that God has given to those who will seek it.

Sunset at the Red Sea.

Chapter 11

Judean Hills and The Shephelah

Hebron

World's Oldest Lived-in City: In ancient times, those seeking the spirit of God lived in the mountains near Jerusalem and Bethlehem. Close to Bethlehem is Hebron—the world's oldest, continuously-inhabited city. In archaeological excavations, over a hundred thousand pots and pottery pieces were discovered. Buildings predating the pyramids have also been identified.

Abraham at Hebron: More than one hundred levels of civilization have been identified, one of which is from the time of Abraham who was a prince there. He purchased the cave of Machpelah in Hebron in which to bury his descendants.

> *And Abraham stood up from before his dead, and spake unto the sons of Heth, saying,*
>
> *I am a stranger and a sojourner with you: give me a possession of a burying place with you, that I may bury my dead out of my sight.*
>
> *... and intreat for me to Ephron the son of Zohar,*
>
> *That he may give me the cave of Machpelah, which he hath, which is in the end of his field; for as much money as it is worth he shall give it me for a possession of a burying place amongst you. GENESIS 23:3-4, 8-9*

Abraham led a small army from Hebron to protect Lot, his nephew, living at Sodom about sixty miles away.

> *And when Abram heard that his brother was taken captive, he armed his trained servants, born in his own house, three hundred and eighteen, and pursued them unto Dan. GENESIS 14:14*

King David's Capital: Hebron was David's capital when he was king of the tribe of Judah. Later, Jerusalem was the capital of all of Israel when David became king over all the tribes of Israel,

---

"Before this dramatic event, the selection of David to be a king was somewhat difficult for the prophet Samuel."

Abraham's Tomb at Hebron.

In Hebron he reigned over Judah seven years and six months: and in Jerusalem he reigned thirty and three years over all Israel and Judah.   2 SAMUEL 5:5

Today's Jews and Arabs in Hebron: In modern times, Hebron has been a seat of Jewish learning. This continued until the "Arab Massacres" of 1929 and 1936 when it became an entirely Arab city and remained so until 1967. That is when Jewish settlers once again established nearby Kiryat Arba.

The modern-day attraction for Jews and Arabs in Hebron is the tomb of Machpelah, where the traditional tombs of father Abraham and his wife Sarah, their son Isaac and his wife Rebekah, and their son Jacob (Israel) and his wife Leah are located. During the sixth and seventh centuries, Arabs turned the Herodian monumental building into a mosque, but recently Jews have rebuilt a synagogue in part of the complex.

The current political uncertainties and sporadic conflicts between Arabs and Jews are quite unlike the centuries of cooperation that Arabs and Jews have had in this ancient city. The one unifying factor could be the link to Abraham, grandfather of both Jews and Arabs.

Primitive and Modern Contrasts: The contrasts of being able to view both primitive and modern lifestyles, seeing modern structures sandwiched between the many layers of old buildings, as well as pondering ancient history while observing events unfold in the present, bring one a sense of amazement that the city of Hebron has existed uninterrupted since the beginning of civilization.

Valley of Elah

David and Goliath: East of Hebron is the Valley of Elah. *Elah* is the Hebrew name for the terebinth trees, which now are growing again as they did in the times of the Kingdom of Israel. Before the first kingdom of Israel was fully established, the Philistines, still maintaining their stronghold at Azekah, sent a cursing giant to intimidate the Israelites. Forty days of badgering and minor skirmishes did not soften the Israelites' stand; they would not give up the Valley of Elah leading up to Bethlehem and Jerusalem. A young shepherd boy, visiting his brothers at the front, saw and heard Goliath. By this time, young David had already been ordained King of Israel by the prophet Samuel (in obscurity and without public knowledge). When David heard and saw Goliath and then saw the men of Israel retreat in fear, he volunteered to remove this menace from them. David said to Saul,

> *...The Lord that delivered me out of the paw of the lion, and out of the paw of the bear, he will deliver me out of the hand of this Philistine....*
>
> *[Then, David] ...chose him five smooth stones out of the brook...*
> *1 SAMUEL 17:37,40 (also see 1-51)*

David took just one stone and struck Goliath in the head. It is obvious in the reading of this account that David killed Goliath with a sling and a stone. To make it more obvious, he cut off his head. But more important is the quiet implication that he conquered Goliath with his faith in the Lord, relying on the spirit that led him.

This old Arab bus ran between Jerusalem and Hebron. Hebron is the world's oldest, continuously inhabited city, and was King David's capital of Israel before Jerusalem.

David Chosen as King: It is interesting to note that before this dramatic event, the selection of David to be a king was somewhat difficult for the prophet Samuel. King Saul had turned from his righteous ways;

> *And the Lord said unto Samuel, How long wilt thou mourn for Saul, seeing I have rejected him from reigning over Israel? fill thine horn with oil, and go, I will send thee to Jesse the Bethlehemite: for I have provided me a king among his sons.*
>
> *And Samuel said, How can I go? if Saul hear it, he will kill me. And the Lord said, Take an heifer with thee, and say, I am come to sacrifice to the Lord.*
>
> *And call Jesse to the sacrifice, and I will shew thee what thou shalt do: and thou shalt anoint unto me him whom I name unto thee.*
> *1 SAMUEL 16:1-3*

Then the Lord gave some profound advice and insight to Samuel (which we could take to heart):

> *Look not on his countenance, or on the height of his stature; ...for the Lord seeth not as man seeth; for man looketh on the outward appearance, but the Lord looketh on the heart.   1 SAMUEL 16:7*

It is human nature to see the obvious, but with God's insight the not-so-obvious qualities, the subtleties, become profound. After interviewing all the obvious sons of Jesse, Samuel asked,

> *...Are here all thy children? And he said, There remaineth yet the youngest, and, behold, he keepeth the sheep. And Samuel said unto Jesse, Send and fetch him: for we will not sit down till he come hither.   1 SAMUEL 16:11*

Samuel was inspired to ordain the shepherd boy David as the next King of Israel.

> *...and the Spirit of the Lord came upon David from that day forward.   1 SAMUEL 16:13*

David, who eventually became the finest and most revered king Israel had, was ordained a king in obscurity and kept his God-given calling quiet until the proper time. His descendant, Jesus of Nazareth, also came from obscurity and kept his holy calling unannounced until the proper time.

Bet Shemesh in the Shephelah

Home of Samson: North of the Valley of Elah is *Bet Shemesh* meaning "House of the Sun." It guards one of the main corridors to Jerusalem. These corridors go up through the foothills of Judea known as the Shephelah. At Bet Shemesh, relics of ancient forms of worship remain visible today, such as a three-stepped altar. This altar is a round platform which is most likely built on top of other religious altars or worship sites. Samson, whose name is derived from *Shemesh*—"the sun"—was

Shepherd boys still roam the hills and valleys
of Israel, much the same as they did
thousands of years ago.

Three-stepped altar at Bet Shemesh. Samson lived in Bet Shemesh (House of the Sun). Samson was a Nazarite priest, but corrupted his calling and later destroyed himself in the act of revenge. Bet Shemesh was an ancient Canaanite town before it was a town of Judah.

born nearby. His parents were promised by God that he would be a priestly, dedicated person throughout his life, a Nazarite chosen to release the Israelites from Philistine bondage. A heaven-sent messenger said,

> *For, lo, thou shalt conceive, and bear a son; and no razor shall come on his head: for the child shall be a Nazarite unto God from the womb: and he shall begin to deliver Israel out of the hand of the Philistines. JUDGES 13:5*

Samson's Folly: Samson abused his God-given strength. As a Nazarite, he was forbidden to kill—except the sacrificial offerings to the Lord—yet he killed a lion and even ate honey from its unclean carcass. This was a mockery to his sacred calling as a priestly Nazarite.

> *Then went Samson down, and his father and his mother, to Timnath, and came to the vineyards of Timnath: and, behold, a young lion roared against him.*
>
> *And he rent him as he would have rent a kid, and he had nothing in his hand: but he told not his father or his mother what he had done.*
>
> *...and after a time...he turned aside to see the carcase of the lion: and, behold, there was a swarm of bees and honey in the carcase of the lion.*
>
> *And he took thereof in his hands, and went on eating, and came to his father and mother, and he gave them, and they did eat: but he told not them that he had taken the honey out of the carcase of the lion. JUDGES 14:5-6, 8-9*

Samson married a Philistine and mocked the God-given gift of strength he had. He also had fits of anger, during which he killed many people. It has been said that he killed people just to get the "shirts off their backs." Remember, he killed thirty men in Ashkelon to pay the Philistines the garments he had wagered in a riddle.

> *And Samson's wife wept before him, and said, Thou dost but hate me, and lovest me not: thou hast put forth a riddle unto the children of my people, and hast not told it me....*
>
> *And she wept before him...and it came to pass...that he told her... and she told the riddle to the children of her people.*
>
> *And the men of the city said unto him on the seventh day before the sun went down, What is sweeter than honey? and what is stronger than a lion? And he said unto them, If ye had not plowed with my heifer, ye had not found out my riddle.*
>
> *...and he went down to Ashkelon, and slew thirty men of them, and took their spoil, and gave change of garments unto them which expounded the riddle.... JUDGES 14:16-19*

Samson Betrayed by Pride: Samson mocked God by assuming that his strength was his own doing. Even when he revealed to Delilah that his strength came from being a Nazarite, he no longer believed that the gift came from God.

> *And she said unto him, How canst thou say, I love thee, when thine heart is not with me? thou hast mocked me these three times, and hast not told me wherein thy great strength lieth.*
>
> *. . . he told her all his heart, and said . . . There hath not come a razor upon mine head; for I have been a Nazarite unto God from my mother's womb: if I be shaven, then my strength will go from me, and I shall become weak, and be like any other man. . . .*
>
> *And she said, The Philistines be upon thee, Samson. And he awoke out of his sleep, and said, I will go out as at other times before, and shake myself. And he wist not that the Lord was departed from him.* JUDGES 16:15-20

The Philistines finally had their tormentor; he was blinded and bound like a donkey to a millstone. Yet the Lord would use him once again.

> *But the Philistines took him, and put out his eyes, and brought him down to Gaza, and bound him with fetters of brass; and he did grind in the prison house.*
>
> *Howbeit the hair of his head began to grow again after he was shaven.*
>
> *Then the lords of the Philistines gathered them together for...a great sacrifice unto Dagon their god....And when the people saw him [Samson], they praised their god...*
>
> *...And they called for Samson out of the prison house; and he made them sport: and they set him between the pillars.*
>
> *And Samson said unto the lad that held him by the hand, Suffer me that I may feel the pillars whereupon the house standeth, that I may lean upon them.*
>
> *Now the house was full of men and women; and all the lords of the Philistines were there; and there were upon the roof about three thousand men and women...* JUDGES 16:21-27

Samson's Revenge: Then Samson cried to the Lord. His prayer was a pitiful, self-serving call for vengeance. Samson had not learned from his past experience.

> *And Samson called unto the Lord, and said, O Lord GOD, remember me, I pray thee, and strengthen me, I pray thee, only this once, O God, that I may be at once avenged of the Philistines for my two eyes....*

...David picked up five stones from a dried
brook in the valley of Elah.

> *And Samson said, Let me die with the Philistines. And he bowed himself with all his might; and the house fell upon the lords, and upon all the people that were therein. So the dead which he slew at his death were more than they which he slew in his life.*
>
> *Then his brethren and all the house of his father came down, and took him, and brought him up, and buried him between Zorah and Eshtaol in the burying place of Manoah his father. And he judged Israel twenty years.   JUDGES 16:28-31*

Although he was a judge in Israel for twenty years and broke the Philistine hold on Israel, he died miserably. As one reflects over the life of Samson, it seems that God kept his promise of breaking the Philistine hold on the Israelites, even though Samson did not keep his promise to be a dedicated priest and an honorable judge in Israel. He died to avenge his lost eyesight by killing others. Yet his brothers brought him to his family's homestead. Samson was buried in his father's grave, located in one of the canyons leading up to Jerusalem.

Up to Jerusalem

Six Canyons Lead to Jerusalem: As was indicated in Chapter 9, Jerusalem of today is like the palm of your right hand that is facing up. However, the Old City is just a thumbprint in size. The five fingers and the wrist to the elbow represent the six canyons or corridors that lead "up to Jerusalem." At the top, middle, and bottom of each of these six finger-like canyons are fortress-like or hilltop settlements that guard the approaches to the Holy City. Most of these settlements are at the same locations as were the ancient, biblical sites.

> *Moreover he built cities in the mountains of Judah, and in the forests he built castles and towers.   2 CHRONICLES 27:4*

Bab El-Wad: The strongest and most important canyon leading to and from Jerusalem is known as the Corridor, or in Arabic the Bab El-Wad. In the 1948 struggle for independence, the first Prime Minister, David Ben-Gurion, ordered that Jerusalem must be kept open and available to Jews. The Arabs set out to besiege the Holy City by blocking this and other canyons.

Independence and the "Burma Road" of Jerusalem: When the Bab El-Wad was blocked, the Jews dug another precarious route through a nearby canyon. That was popularly dubbed the "Burma Road" in the media. American volunteer Mickey Markus engineered the Burma Road and then was killed accidentally by a security guard on the very day of its completion. A motion picture called "Cast a Giant Shadow" was produced; it follows the story of the construction of the Burma Road. The relics of the Israeli tractors, trucks and vehicles that were ambushed in 1948 are still left today at the roadside as memorials of the struggle for independence.

David made quite an impression on Goliath on that fateful day at Azekah, a hill overlooking the valley of Elah.

Unfinished watchtower in the Judean Hills.

SCRIPTURAL REFERENCES (KJV)

Section Three

Features of Ancient Jerusalem

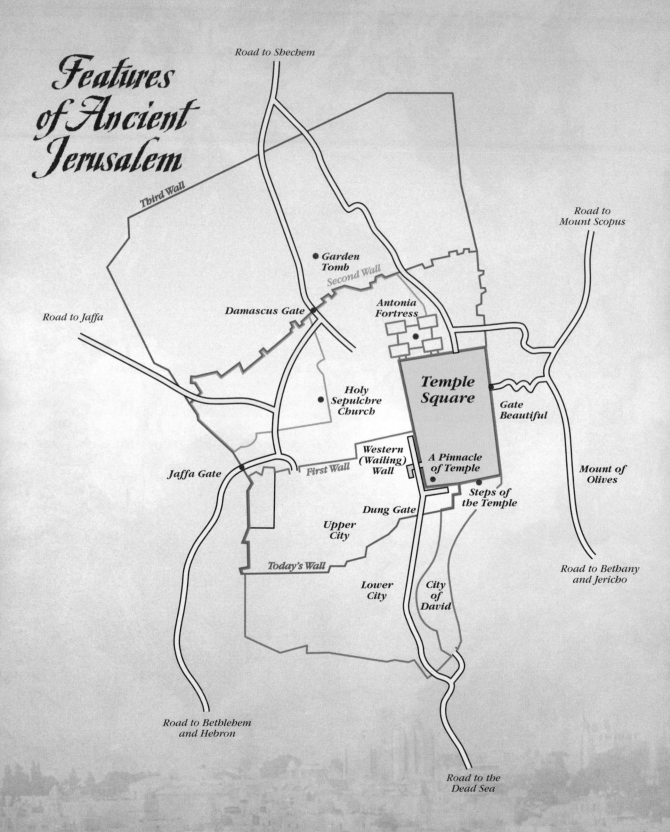

Road to Shechem

Third Wall

Road to Mount Scopus

Garden Tomb

Second Wall

Road to Jaffa

Damascus Gate

Antonia Fortress

Holy Sepulchre Church

Temple Square

Gate Beautiful

Western (Wailing) Wall

A Pinnacle of Temple

Mount of Olives

Jaffa Gate

First Wall

Dung Gate

Steps of the Temple

Upper City

Road to Bethany and Jericho

Today's Wall

Lower City

City of David

Road to Bethlehem and Hebron

Road to the Dead Sea

- *Overview* -
Jerusalem's Holy Places

We will explore the **MODEL CITY**, a half-acre miniature representation of **JERUSALEM** as it was two thousand years ago. This will increase your understanding of **ISRAEL'S HOLY TEMPLE**. The present-day **OLD CITY** still has many features similar to those of ancient Jerusalem. Amazing ancient customs remain today. For example, **MONEY CHANGERS** are still plying the streets close to the temple area. A **PINNACLE** of the **TEMPLE SQUARE** has been rediscovered. The **DOME OF THE ROCK** and the **WESTERN (WAILING) WALL** are still used for traditional worship practices by Moslems and Jews. These practices still resemble those performed in ancient temple rites. Places used for ancient **SACRIFICES**, **WASHINGS** and **ANOINTINGS** are still most revealing. Recent findings may have clearly identified the **HOLY OF HOLIES**. Evidence of Christian traditions as old as 16-17 hundred years can be discovered in the **OLD CITY**. The best known is the **CHURCH OF THE HOLY SEPULCHER**, housing orthodox churches that venerate this as the place of Jesus' crucifixion and burial. Their different calendars, cultural conflicts, and competition are in stark contrast to the holy events and reverence they espouse.

There are four sets of steps and pillars leading up to the Dome of the Rock in Jerusalem. The dome has religious significance for the Moslems. They believe that it will play a role in the last judgment of mankind.

Chapter 12

The Holy City

Stumbling Blocks or Stepping Stones

 A wise man once said, "On the pathway of life, many people stumble across the truth, pick themselves up and keep right on going." In this land of Israel, many events were revealed from heaven. To some, these events may appear as stumbling blocks, while others accept them as spiritual experiences. We can also consider the thousands of details in the ancient scriptures that deal with covenants, signs, and tokens. Some or all of these details might be confusing unless a key is discovered, a way of understanding how, when, where they occurred and what they meant.

Learning About Holy Places: In Jerusalem's Old City, we can examine details and events that deal with places just a few hundred yards apart. It is interesting to compare the ancient prophecies with historical fulfillment and see how locations reveal much about the events that took place there. Most of the people in the land of Israel find little or no meaning in the Christian "holy places." Because some sites are spurious, the authentic ones are often not even considered. Let us learn about places that were specially set apart for events that would influence people eternally. In that way, the sites and considerations of the symbolism of past traditions may teach us what to expect in the future. Also, metaphors become more understandable and meaningful for our daily lives.

"Let us learn about places that were specially set apart for events that would influence people eternally."

The Model City of Jerusalem

The Temple: To understand the Holy Temple of Jerusalem, we'll first examine the model city. It is an accurate miniature of ancient Jerusalem the way it was two thousand years ago. If you were as small as your thumb, you could wander through the mini-city as you might wander through the real city of Jerusalem. Great effort has been made to re-create the physical features as they were in times past. This model city was built by a father as a memorial to his son who died in the 1948 War of Independence.

Model Changes Constantly: The model is constantly being changed as new archaeological discoveries are made in Jerusalem. Viewing the temple model as it was and understanding what it was used for lays the groundwork for a better appreciation of temples and the Jerusalem temple site today. This will also help you understand the importance of Jerusalem and its holy places.

Temple Square

Outline Still Visible: The model city clearly shows the major edifice of the city two millennia ago as the Temple Square. On the Temple Mount today stands the Dome of the Rock, a Moslem shrine. However, the general outline of the ancient Jewish temple area is still recognizable.

Three Courtyards: One can still see the remains of the three courtyards. The outer courtyard was for the general population (in Herod's time, even non-Jews were allowed in this courtyard). The middle courtyard was under the direction of twelve priests. The innermost courtyard was under the direction of the High Priest. One can also make an approximate guess as to where the inner courtyard or Holy of Holies might have been. About forty acres was the size of the ancient temple, including the courtyards. In fact, it was an outdoor temple. Religious functions and rituals occurred in open, outdoor worship areas as well as within the buildings.

The Crowded Temple City

Many Inhabitants of Jerusalem: Jerusalem two thousand years ago was much larger than what is contained within the walled Old City of today. It contained almost two-thirds more area and more than double the population of today. In those days, there were about eighty thousand inhabitants. However, another hundred to a hundred and fifty thousand or more visitors came during the major holy days. They included Passover in the spring, Succoth in the fall, Yom Kippur, Rosh Hashanah, and so on. Today, around thirty thousand people live within the walled Old City, but more than six hundred thousand others live outside of it.

Temple Building Program: During the life of Herod the Great when Jesus of Nazareth came to Judea, a great building program was under way on the ancient site of Solomon's Temple. The outer city wall and the Temple were only completed a generation later, about thirty years after Jesus' death.

Destruction by Titus: Only six years later, in A.D. 70, this beautiful city was destroyed by Titus; all of the buildings and courtyards of the Temple were demolished and burned. Only three towers Herod the Great had built remained. (They were built in memory of his wife, brother, and friend whom he had killed.) Great heaps of earth covered the once holy city; as an insult, salt was poured on the earth-covered ruins so that even the persevering lilies of the field could not grow. (These "lilies" actually are deep red anemones, poppy-like flowers that manage to grow almost anywhere in the spring months.) Herod had not foreseen such destruction as he carefully built massive city walls and used the natural landscape to protect himself and secure the city.

The Model City is an accurate miniature model of Jerusalem as it was two thousand years ago. It is constantly being changed as new archaeological discoveries are made. The model was built by a father as a memorial to his son who died in the 1948 War of Independence.

Years ago, Jews would throw rocks at Absalom's tomb in the Kidron Valley because Absalom did not honor his father, David. It is said that some Jewish mothers have brought their children here to remind them of what can happen to rebellious youth.

Valleys to Protect the Temple City

Gehenna, Valley of Hell: On the west and south of Jerusalem's city wall was a ravine used as an exit for sewage and a place to burn waste and garbage. In very early times, people were even burned in this valley as sacrifices to pagan gods.

> *Moreover he burnt incense in the valley of the son of Hinnom, and burnt his children in the fire, after the abominations of the heathen whom the Lord had cast out before the children of Israel.*
> *2 CHRONICLES 28:3*

The constant odor, smoke, and fire gave it the name of *Hinnom* that in ancient Hebrew meant "hell." In modern Hebrew, the word for hell is *Gehinom*. In English the term Valley of Gehenna was the transliteration of the Aramaic *Gai Hinom*, "valley of hell."

Kidron Valley: On the eastern side of the city's wall is a ravine known as the Kidron. Due to the deepness of both valleys, the Gehenna and the Kidron provided an excellent defense system of the city walls high above.

> *Now after this he built a wall without the city of David, on the west side of Gihon, in the valley, even to the entering in at the fish gate, and compassed about Ophel, and raised it up a very great height, and put captains of war in all the fenced cities of Judah.*
> *2 CHRONICLES 33:14*

If an enemy attempted an attack from the east, south, or west sides of the city, they lost all the elements of surprise. They had the disadvantage of fighting and climbing upwards at the same time.

A Stone Quarry: The area north of the city did not have a ravine, so during various centuries one was created by carving a stone quarry. Incidentally, the stone from the quarry was used to build the temple. To carry the symbolism a little further, the temple was used to teach about the Atonement. The Atonement was completed in the quarry. Later it became the Place of a Skull—the crucifixion site.

Northern Walls: Several east-west walls were also built on the north part of the city to hinder a possible attack from the north. The first northern wall was built before Herod's time. He added to it, and it became a bridge. This extended from his palace on the west side of the city to the temple on the east side of the city.

The first wall, as it was known, went eastward from Herod's palace and crossed the north-south Tyropeon Valley that was immediately west of the Temple Square. That wall was also the bridge for the priestly people of the "Upper City" to get to the temple. From the ravine's depth, the temple's western walls rose to heights of as much as a few hundred feet in some places. This first-wall bridge was an essential structure for the priestly residents who used it as a convenient entrance to the temple. Most of them lived in the western part of the city overlooking the temple.

The Place of Crucifixion

The second northern wall was farther north of the bridge and reflected the growing nature of the Holy City. It was constructed and in place by the time Jesus was crucified. Since in New Testament times crucifixions were outside the walls of the city, it is very likely referring to the second wall. As previously stated, many feel that the crucifixion site was in the quarry, just outside the second wall. It was at the site of a sheer cliff face that still looms above the rock excavations. Even today, that site is known as a place of execution.

Also a Place of Stoning: Anciently, Jews were stoned by toppling the victim down a cliff to his death and then covering the body with stones. That always had to be done outside the city walls. It can be assumed that the Romans may have used the same place as a site for crucifixion.

> *...Naboth did blaspheme God and the king. Then they carried him forth out of the city, and stoned him with stones, that he died.* 1 KINGS 21:13

> *And cast him out of the city, and stoned him: and the witnesses laid down their clothes at a young man's feet, whose name was Saul.* ACTS 7:58

> *Wherefore Jesus also, that he might sanctify the people with his own blood, suffered without the gate.* HEBREWS 13:12

Holy Sepulcher Church

Traditional Site of Jesus' Burial: The oldest Christian traditional site of the crucifixion and burial of Jesus is marked by the Church of the Holy Sepulcher. It is west of Temple Square and is within the walls of the city today. There is more interesting information about this site in Chapter 14. However, as mentioned, there is another newer discovery of a "Garden Tomb" that reveals earlier Christian tradition. This discovery casts doubt in some people's minds as to the authenticity of the Sepulcher Church being the place where Jesus was buried and resurrected.

Garden Tomb

Rediscovered Site for Jesus' Burial: Many modern Christians, as well as key figures in the LDS Church, feel that another location, the Garden Tomb, is more likely the correct site of the burial and resurrection of Jesus. This site is north of the Temple Square and outside the present-day wall. This site is near a visible place that resembles a skull. (The crucifixion happened at a place of a skull, and the tomb was in a garden nearby.) It was rediscovered about a hundred years ago. We will later examine this site more closely.

The Western Wall is a part of the ancient
wall that surrounded the temple built at the
time of Herod. The wall is a holy place of
prayer for Jews from all over the world.

Mount Moriah

The Temple Mount: As mentioned earlier, running through the middle of the city was another smaller ravine known in New Testament times as the "Valley of the Cheese Makers," or Tyropeon Valley. Between the Tyropean and the Kidron rose a long, banana-shaped mount called by many different names: Mount Zion, Mount of the Lord, Mount Moriah, and today—the Temple Mount. On it was a great Temple Square. It had structures and meeting areas for temple worship. Religious Jews feel that some time in the future temple worship will be restored in this same area.

> *Then Solomon began to build the house of the Lord at Jerusalem*
> *in mount Moriah, where the Lord appeared unto David his father,*
> *in the place that David had prepared in the threshing floor of*
> *Ornan the Jebusite.   2 CHRONICLES 3:1*

Levite Entrances: In New Testament times, the western wall of the Temple had four entrances used by priests and their families. The first entrance that was northernmost was a private corridor with access to and from the priestly courtyard of the temple. It was for the High Priest.

Herod's Entrance: Another access was the first-wall bridge entrance that led from Herod's palace and over the Tyropeon Valley into Temple Square; Herod and the priests accompanying him used this entrance.

Excavation Problems: It appears that the remains of the High Priest's entrance and the first-wall bridge entrance have been found in recent excavations. What might have been the High Priest's corridor has been closed for now. Because the Orthodox Jews have concerns about priestly rights of even going on the Temple Mount, they presently make no effort to enter. Another reason they do not go there is the Moslem concern about a Jewish presence on the Mount. Much of the wall-bridge leading up to the temple has been destroyed and is now covered with subsequent civilizations and their buildings. Recent excavations reveal some archways—still intact—that supported this wall bridge.

The Women Priests' Gate: The third ancient western gate to the Temple was what the Jews called the Women Priests' Gate. (Levite women did serve in temple functions.)

The Grand Entrance: The fourth entrance was the grand staircase at the southwest corner of Temple Square. No evidence has been found of the women's entrance, but in the nineteenth century, the noted archaeologist Dr. Edward Robinson identified ruins of the fourth grand entrance. Almost a hundred years later, excavations have revealed the foundation of the grand staircase.

Thus, out of the four known ancient gates in the Western Wall, only three have been identified. Newer gates are above them, and at least one of them was just identified as being directly above the bridge entrance that led from Herod's palace. Excavations by this gate reveal an original Herodian entrance and walkway.

Dome of the Rock on the ancient temple mount.

Daniel revealing ancient Jewish temple customs.

The So-Called Wailing Wall

Wailing or Worshiping: In the model city, a red arrow on the temple's Western Wall shows where today's so-called Wailing Wall is situated. Many say that non-Jews have named the wall the Wailing Wall possibly because they have mistaken Jewish prayers as crying or wailing.

Remnant of Western Wall: The worship area of the Wailing Wall is only a remnant of the entire Western Wall. Jews still gather at the wall to worship because they believe they have no priestly permission or authority to go on the Temple Mount itself. The wall serves as the closest gathering spot available. It conveniently serves to somewhat satisfy their yearning to connect with their past. Weddings and Bar Mitzvah celebrations regularly take place here. All of this activity is done in remembrance of similar situations that took place in the Temple, above the wall, before its destruction.

The Wall Desecrated: This Jewish and Christian worship area was desecrated by Moslems throughout the centuries. Much desecration occurred between the years of 1948 and 1967 when Jews were forbidden to enter the Old City or to worship at the wall. Hovels and huts crowded the area up to the wall, and a part of the wall area was used for public toilets. Prior to 1948 when Jerusalem was divided, the wall was available for Jewish worship in some respect or another. The following nineteen years were the only time that access to the wall was completely forbidden (or unavailable).

The Wall Restored: The Israeli armed forces opened the city of Jerusalem again during the Six-Day War. Then the access to the wall was cleared, and it was cleaned. In 1967 Jerusalem again became an open city for worshippers of all faiths. Jews have kept a constant vigil at the wall ever since. At any hour of the day or night, one is likely to find someone there, praying or reciting scriptures.

A view of the Temple Mount on Mount Moriah from the buildings above. The grounds cover about 40 acres and once contained Solomon's temple. This small plot of land is considered sacred for Jews, Moslems, and Christians.

Chapter 13

Temple and Worship Sites

Business at the Southern Wall

 Money Changers and Vendors: The southern area below Temple Square was very busy. People came there to wash and immerse themselves before going into the temple. Stalls with unblemished and washed animals for temple sacrifices were crowded close to and even inside the corridors leading up to the Holy Place. Money changers, anxious to take local and foreign currency in exchange for special temple money that could only be used in the temple, also crowded the entrances to the temple.

Cast Out by Jesus: Jesus cast out all those who bought and sold in the temple and overthrew the tables of the money changers. He said,

> *...Take these things hence; make not my Father's house an house of merchandise.   JOHN 2:16*

Later he cried out,

> *...ye have made it a den of thieves.   MATTHEW 21:13*
> *(see also 12-16)*

Money Changers Today: Money changers still ply the streets of Jerusalem. It seems that foreign currency is still in demand. This practice, along with the continual selling of doves and chicks, seems to make the past ever so present, though the religious purposes of dove offerings are not being fulfilled.

Temptation of Jesus at the Temple Pinnacle

Archaeological Evidence: Recent archaeological discoveries reveal the southwest corner of Temple Square to be the pinnacle where Jesus was tempted to cast himself down so that many people could view a miracle. (Christian tradition incorrectly names the southeast corner as the pinnacle.)

> *Then the devil taketh him up into the holy city, and setteth him on a pinnacle of the temple,   MATTHEW 4:5*

"The unusual red-calf sacrifice in ancient days may have been a foreshadowing of the second messianic appearance on the Mount of Olives in latter days."

A stone was found at the base of the southwest corner of Temple Square. It had writing on it indicating a pulpit or place for the trumpeter or shofar blower. According to Jewish history, that usually occurred at the pinnacle or corner of the temple.

The Gate Beautiful

The Gate of Mercy and Forgiveness: The temple's eastern wall had one entrance reserved for the Messiah's entry. This Gate Beautiful was also known as the Gate of Mercy and as the Gate of Forgiveness.

Yom Kippur—The Day of Atonement: In ancient days, once a year on Yom Kippur—the Day of Atonement—an unblemished, firstborn lamb or goat would be allowed to escape through this gate. It was first "blessed" with the sins of the congregation. The priest would have had to interview the congregation, probably individually. Their confessions of mistakes or experiences of grief and tragedy would then be repeated vocally by the priest as he laid them on the head of the firstborn, unblemished offering.

The Scapegoat for Sins: The effect of hearing the sins repeated and visually seeing them laid on a lamb or goat may have spiritually moved the participants. They were to see, hear, and feel their sins being taken away. So, bearing the sins of the multitude, this scapegoat truly became a symbol of a redeemer to come to take away the sins of the people.

> *And Aaron shall lay both his hands upon the head of the live goat, and confess over him all the iniquities of the children of Israel, and all their transgressions in all their sins, putting them upon the head of the goat, and shall send him away by the hand of a fit man into the wilderness:*
>
> *And the goat shall bear upon him all their iniquities unto a land not inhabited: and he shall let go the goat in the wilderness.*
> LEVITICUS 16:21-22

A Crimson Symbol: Tradition relates that the scapegoat was marked with a crimson ribbon to indicate that it was an animal not to be killed. It was to die on its own, outside the temple. This is yet another symbol of the Messiah, who would take the sins upon himself and would die on his own outside the temple. His experience of taking sins upon himself would render him red. He would bleed from every pore.

Sacrifice of the Red Calf

Information on the sacrifice of a red calf and on other little-known subjects awaits discovery. The red calf is called a red heifer in the English translation of the Bible.

Sacrificed on the Mount of Olives: According to the Bible and to Jewish customs, the Gate Beautiful was also an exit for the unblemished, firstborn, totally red-haired calf. According to well-documented traditions, the red calf was led across the Kidron Valley and up the Mount of Olives. It was then sacrificed high enough to be over the temple yet in a straight line with the Gate Beautiful and still be northward of the altar.

The so-called "Golden Gate" or Gate Beautiful stands on the site of the gate that Jesus entered when He came to Jerusalem in triumph during the last week of His life. The gate was closed and walled up by the Turks in 1530.

Ashes Used for Purification: The red calf would be totally burned and its ashes used in special immersion ceremonies for the purification of sins.

> *This is the ordinance...which the Lord hath commanded,...bring thee a red heifer without spot, wherein is no blemish...*
>
> *And ye shall give her unto Eleazar the priest, that he may bring her forth without the camp [Temple], and one shall slay her...*
>
> *And one shall burn the heifer in his sight;...*
>
> *...And a man that is clean shall gather up the ashes of the heifer,... and it shall be kept for the congregation of the children of Israel for a water of separation: it is a purification for sin...*
> *NUMBERS 19:2-10*

Religious Jews still immerse themselves for ritual purification. However, one of the reasons they do not immerse for purification of sins in a separate font is because they do not have ashes of a red calf.

A Foreshadowing of the Messiah: The unusual red-calf sacrifice in ancient days may have been a foreshadowing of the second messianic appearance on the Mount of Olives in latter days. That is when the Messiah will arrive dressed in red.

> *Who is this that cometh from Edom, with dyed garments from Bozrah? this that is glorious in his apparel, travelling in the greatness of his strength? I that speak in righteousness, mighty to save.*
>
> *Wherefore art thou red in thine apparel, and thy garments like him that treadeth in the winefat?   ISAIAH 63:1-2*
>
> *And it shall be said: Who is this that cometh down from God in heaven with dyed garments; yea, from the regions which are not known, clothed in his glorious apparel, traveling in the greatness of his strength?*
>
> *And he shall say: I am he who spake in righteousness, mighty to save.*
>
> *And the Lord shall be red in his apparel, and his garments like him that treadeth in the wine-vat.*
> *DOCTRINE & COVENANTS 133:46-48*

Blood from Every Pore: The suffering of Jesus as he bled from every pore for the sins of all people is incomprehensible.

> *And being in an agony he prayed more earnestly: and his sweat was as it were great drops of blood falling down to the ground.*
> *LUKE 22:44*
>
> *Which suffering caused myself, even God, the greatest of all, to tremble because of pain, and to bleed at every pore, and to suffer both body and spirit—and would that I might not drink the bitter cup, and shrink.   DOCTRINE & COVENANTS 19:18*

The Western Wall was sometimes called the "Wailing Wall" because Jews sorrowed over the loss of their temple. However, the nation of Israel is now restored and today's Jews come to the wall in thankful prayer and rejoicing.

The Chosen Site: That suffering, surely marked by red-stained clothing, occurred on the Mount of Olives east of the Gate Beautiful. It probably happened high on the mount and in line with the spot just north of the temple altar. The sites of the Mount of Olives and the Temple Mount (Moriah) were apparently chosen long in advance for significant events of salvation.

The Red Calf and the Messiah, a Chiasmus: A red calf and the coming of the Messiah in red—on the Mount of Olives—create a significant chiasmus again. In ancient days, a red calf was offered on the Mount of Olives for forgiveness of sin. In latter days the Messiah, the atoner for sins, will appear on the same Mount of Olives dressed in red. The center of the chiasmus points to Jesus' suffering and bleeding for the sins of all people while he was on the Mount of Olives in the meridian of time.

Reviving Ancient Temple Customs: Today there is a small group of Orthodox Jews (mostly Levites) who call themselves the "Temple Mount Faithful." They are hoping to find a way to raise a completely red-haired, firstborn, unblemished calf. This is in expectation of immersion for purification of sins that would precede the building of the temple again. They are also sewing clothing, aprons, and robes, and designing artifacts like the ones used in the temple anciently.

Biblical Sacrifices

Study of ancient biblical sacrifices is not usually considered exciting reading. The Bible has many details that in today's cultures seem unnecessary. Let's examine a few details and see if we can relate the symbolism and meaning to our modern religious understanding.

Abraham's Sacrifices: Twenty centuries before Jesus, Abraham, living in the Ur of Chaldees, had a difficult relationship with his father, Terah, who was taken in by the idol worshiping prevalent in that area. Various gods were idolized, as people made statues and doted on works of wood and metal. (Add glass to the wood and metal, and it might look like a TV today!) Idol worshiping included human sacrifice. Abraham was about to be offered when at the last moment the real God, the Father in Heaven, saved him from that pagan practice. God brought him out of the land of the Chaldees to the Crossroads of the East. There Abraham was to have a great family.

> *And the Lord said unto Abram, . . .*
>
> *And I will make thy seed as the dust of the earth: so that if a man can number the dust of the earth, then shall thy seed also be numbered.   GENESIS 13:14-16*

Some might consider it unfortunate (or even a mistake), that he married a woman, although very beautiful, who could not bear children. After years of pleading with the Lord and then with the Lord's permission, Sarah gave Abraham her handmaid, Hagar, who bore a son named Ishmael, which means "heard of God." Later he married Keturah who bore six children. They began to fulfill the prophecy of a great posterity.

...and Abram called his son's name, which Hagar bare, Ishmael.
GENESIS 16:15

Then again Abraham took a wife, and her name was Keturah.

And she bare him Zimran, and Jokshan, and Medan, and Midian,
and Ishbak, and Shuah.   GENESIS 25:1-2

The Arabs are considered descendants of Hagar. It is also a possibility that the Bedouin and the Druze of today may have descended from Keturah and her six children.

A Miracle Son: When Sarah was ninety years old, an angel appeared to Abraham to announce that she would yet bear a son. Apparently she laughed; surely she at ninety and Abraham at ninety-nine could not have a child! (Can you imagine what the neighbors might have said?) However, the impossible became possible, and God blessed them exceedingly. They had a son (an only son between them), which they named *Yitzhak* (Isaac in English), which means "laughter, joy."

Therefore Sarah laughed within herself, saying, After I am waxed
old shall I have pleasure, my lord being old also?

And the Lord said unto Abraham, Wherefore did Sarah laugh,
saying, Shall I of a surety bear a child, which am old?
GENESIS 18:12-13

Raising this miracle child must have been a great joy. Jewish rabbinical tradition tells us that Isaac was in his early thirties when God commanded Abraham to offer Isaac as a human sacrifice. What a contrast to the very thing that the same God had saved Abraham from years before! Remember, human sacrifice was a pagan custom Abraham had fled from in Ur.

Isaac to be Sacrificed: God instructed Abraham to go to Mount Moriah to sacrifice his firstborn son of Sarah, his wife. Mount Moriah was designated as the place of sacrifice, though it is very close to the Mount of Olives which is much higher. High places were usually selected as sacrificial locations. The name Moriah is derived from the words *moreh*, "teacher", and *Yah*, the shortened version of the word "Jehovah." Names ending with the sound "ah" often refer to Jehovah, such as Elijah, Micah, Hezekiah, Jeremiah, Isaiah, and so on. The word Jehovah is not spoken in Hebrew, since it means *"I AM."* There is also no conjugation of the words to be in the first person. ("I am" is not spoken in Hebrew.) So, Mount Moriah may mean "to be taught of Jehovah." This is an appropriate metaphor, a lesson giving us insight to this unusual event.

Sacrifices were accomplished by quickly drawing the blade across the blood and breath of an unblemished, firstborn animal. This was the biblical instruction and probably the most humane way of rendering the animal lifeless.

An Angel Stops the Sacrifice: Before the blood and breath of Isaac was taken, an angel commanded Abraham to stop. God would provide a lamb for the sacrifice. Abraham and Isaac found a substitute ram in the thicket and offered it instead.

And Abraham stretched forth his hand, and took the knife to
slay his son.

Some scholars feel that the actual Garden of Gethsemene was located higher on the Mount of Olives than the traditional spot. This is near where the red calf was traditionally sacrificed according to scripture and Jewish custom.

And the angel of the Lord called unto him out of heaven, and said,...

... Lay not thine hand upon the lad,...

And Abraham lifted up his eyes, and looked, and behold behind him a ram caught in a thicket by his horns: and Abraham went and took the ram, and offered him up for a burnt offering in the stead of his son.   GENESIS 22:10-13

Substitute Sacrifices: From that time on, other substitute animals, always firstborn and unblemished, were sacrificed on Mount Moriah. Interestingly, the sacrifice was always done on the northern side of the temple altar.

And he shall kill it on the side of the altar northward before the Lord: and the priests, Aaron's sons, shall sprinkle his blood round about upon the altar.   LEVITICUS 1:11

The Place of a Skull

A Place of Crucifixion: Today on the northern end of the Temple Mount stands an abandoned quarry with caves that give it a grotesque skull-like look. Many people consider this the Place of a Skull, Calvary or Golgotha. They feel this is where the Lamb of God, the firstborn Son of God, was sacrificed when he was crucified.

And he bearing his cross went forth into a place called the place of a skull, which is called in the Hebrew Golgotha: JOHN 19:17

This Place of a Skull looks like the location described as the crucifixion site in the New Testament. However, some scholars and Christians have only recently recognized and identified it as such. Later, we will discuss it in more detail and also describe an empty first-century Jewish tomb close by.

The Purpose of Temples

The remarkable symbolisms of time, places, and events seemed to have fore-shadowed the Messiah, the Holy One of Israel. Abraham's life was chiastic: First to be offered as a human sacrifice and then to be saved, later to be commanded to offer his own son as a sacrifice and then to have him saved. These events teach us that God, also on Mount Moriah, was to offer his Son as a sacrifice to save us all.

Atonement Instruction: It is apparent that the temple, later built on Mount Moriah, was to teach about the Atonement for all people. It is inevitable that the Savior will return to the house of the Lord and restore it as a place of worship and teaching.

Behold, I will send my messenger, and he shall prepare the way before me: and the Lord, whom ye seek, shall suddenly come to his temple, even the messenger of the covenant, whom ye delight in: behold, he shall come, saith the Lord of hosts.   MALACHI 3:1

Sacrifice: In the past, the temple had an outer courtyard where the people were taught. There was a central courtyard where twelve priests functioned. Then there was an inner courtyard for the ark of the covenant where only the High Priest could enter at appointed times. When the High Priest was ready for another sacrifice in front of the ark, he would light a fire and burn incense. It makes sense that incense was used to offset the odor, as parts of the animal would have to be totally burned. The burning incense signaled the priests in the next courtyard to ready themselves. The twelve priests would don their appropriate clothings, gather their temple instruments, and ring bells to signal the congregation to gather.

A Shepherd's Analogy: The symbolic sequence of the highest priest, twelve high priests, and the congregation are still seen today by the lowly shepherd with his flock. The symbolism speaks volumes. He leads the sheep, with usually about a dozen older sheep. They are the lead sheep that carry bells around their necks. When the shepherd calls, the lead sheep, having more experience than the others, respond first and run toward him. The ringing bells become a signal for the rest of the flock to gather and follow their shepherd. How comforting is the picture in my mind of "The Lord is my Shepherd."

The Ark of the Covenant: The ark of the covenant in the temple also contained the second set of tablets that Moses received from God. He broke the first set when he saw the children of Israel worshiping a golden calf. The ark also held artifacts such as the seven-branched candelabra, *Menorah*, the staff of Aaron, and some manna from the wilderness.

Urim and Thummim: The temple also housed the Urim and Thummim. These were special seer stones used by ancient prophets to discern the truth and receive revelation.

> *...and the ark of the covenant overlaid round about with gold, wherein was the golden pot that had manna, and Aaron's rod that budded, and the tables of the covenant;* HEBREWS 9:4

> *And Aaron shall bear the names of the children of Israel in the breastplate of judgment upon his heart, when he goeth in unto the holy place.. .*

> *And thou shalt put in the breastplate of judgment the Urim and the Thummim; and they shall be upon Aaron's heart, when he goeth in before the Lord: and Aaron shall bear the judgment of the children of Israel upon his heart before the Lord continually* EXODUS 28:29-30

The original ark was lost six hundred years before Herod's temple was built, but its place was reserved for the eventual restoration of all things.

> *Repent ye therefore, and be converted, that your sins may be blotted out, when the times of refreshing shall come from the presence of the Lord;*

*A true shepherd leads his flock of sheep
instead of driving them from behind. This is
a universal image of leadership that was
lovingly taught by the Savior.*

A scale model of the Temple of Herod in Jerusalem. This miniature building is part of a large model of the city of Jerusalem as it was 2000 years ago. The entire model is made of the original materials that were used in ancient Jerusalem.

And he shall send Jesus Christ, which before was preached unto you:

Whom the heaven must receive until the times of restitution of all things, which God hath spoken by the mouth of all his holy prophets since the world began.   ACTS 3:19-21

Temple Restoration

Jews Await Temple Rebuilding: There is still hope among religious Jews that the temple, so utterly destroyed in the year 70 A.D., will be built again. In addition to scriptural prophecies, there are legends and stories that persist with that expectation.

Latter-day Joseph and David: There are rabbinic suggestions of expected heaven-sent visitors that include a latter-day Messiah Ben-Joseph who will receive the keys of the gathering of Israel and restore temple worship. This was referred to by the Chief Rabbi Abraham HaCohen Kook when he explained that the Temple could not be built right away because there was no priesthood. There are other versions of this tradition of a Joseph of latter days. Also, a latter-day David is expected. (This is implied at almost every Bar Mitzvah as the congregants sing "David King of Israel" to the young lad.) Their expectation is of a David who will emerge from obscurity to be a great king or leader in these last days.

> *But they shall serve the Lord their God, and David their king, whom I will raise up unto them.   JEREMIAH 30:9*

> *And I the Lord will be their God, and my servant David a prince among them; I the Lord have spoken it.   EZEKIEL 34:24*

> *Afterward shall the children of Israel return, and seek the Lord their God, and David their king; and shall fear the Lord and his goodness in the latter days.   HOSEA 3:5*

Latter-day scripture refers to the Lord, to the Lord's servant (possibly a latter-day David "on whom there is laid much power"), and to another latter-day servant (Joseph Smith with "keys for the gathering"). These servants are of dual descendancy. These ideas are given as answers to questions from Isaiah Chapter 11.

> *Who is the stem of Jesse?...It is Christ.*

> *What is the rod?...It is a servant in the hands of Christ, who is partly a descendant of Jesse as well as of Ephraim, or of the house of Joseph, on whom there is laid much power.*

> *What is the root of Jesse?... It is a descendant of Jesse, as well as of Joseph, unto whom rightly belongs the priesthood, and the keys of the kingdom, for an ensign, and for the gathering of my people in the last days.   DOCTRINE & COVENANTS 113:1-6*

Moses and Elijah to Return: The well-known anticipated visit of Moses and Elijah also keeps Jewish hopes alive. These hopes are for a restoration of ancient practices and covenants lost since the temple's destruction. Every Passover and Succoth (festivals that commemorate the deliverance of Israel from Egyptian bondage), the doors are left open for Elijah's and/or Moses' return. At Succoth seven different guests are expected. They are called the *Ushpazim*. It is a traditional Jewish expectation that ancient prophets will return. Even specific dates are used as reminders. It is interesting to consider that Moses' and Elijah's return on the Mount of Transfiguration may have happened at Succoth, the festival of "booths" or "tabernacles." It is a holy week commemorating the deliverance of Israel.

> *And was transfigured before them: and his face did shine as the sun, and his raiment was white as the light.*
>
> *And, behold, there appeared unto them Moses and Elias talking with him.*
>
> *Then answered Peter, and said unto Jesus, Lord, it is good for us to be here: if thou wilt, let us make here three tabernacles; one for thee, and one for Moses, and one for Elias [Elijah].* MATTHEW 17:2-4

Moses and Elijah Have Returned: Latter-day Saints believe that the two prophets Elijah and Moses returned on April 3, 1836 (which happened to be Passover that year, another holy week commemorating the deliverance of Israel).

> *...the heavens were again opened to us; and Moses appeared before us, and committed unto us the keys of the gathering of Israel from the four parts of the earth, and the leading of the ten tribes from the land of the north....*
>
> *After this vision had closed, another great and glorious vision burst upon us; for Elijah the prophet, who was taken to heaven without tasting death, stood before us, and said:*
>
> *Behold, the time has fully come, which was spoken of by the mouth of Malachi—testifying that he [Elijah] should be sent, before the great and dreadful day of the Lord come—*
>
> *To turn the hearts of the fathers to the children, and the children to the fathers, lest the whole earth be smitten with a curse—*
>
> *Therefore, the keys of this dispensation are committed into your hands; and by this ye may know that the great and dreadful day of the Lord is near, even at the doors.*
> DOCTRINE & COVENANTS 110:11-16

*Many Jews ceremoniously wash their hands
at the entrance to the Western Wall in
Jerusalem. This may remind them to have
clean hands and a pure heart before
entering that sacred area.*

Temple Mount and the Dome of the Rock

Ishmael Instead of Isaac: Almost seven hundred years after the second temple was destroyed, the Moslems built a magnificent shrine commemorating Abraham's visit to the Mount to offer Ishmael (not Isaac).

Mohammed at Moriah: Moslems also believe that Mohammed ascended to heaven from that rock. There are legends that the rock also began to ascend, so an angel had to push it back down. There is no evidence that Mohammed actually traveled to the rock in Jerusalem. The rock outcropping under the Dome is simply part of the mountain rather than a separate rock. The Dome of the Rock was completed in 691 A.D. and was built as a shrine instead of a worship center, as mosques are.

Modern Moslem Worship: However, in modern times, remodeling has introduced some "niches" built in the direction of Mecca. It has now become a shrine where Moslems can pray individually, using the niches or alcoves as a directional pointer to Mecca. Chapter 16 has additional details about Moslems' worship practices and building use.

Al Aksa Mosque

The Al Aksa Mosque was built for Moslem group worship. They follow a pattern of exercising and praying which was taught hundreds of years ago by the Dervishes. Today Dervishes are still known for their gyrations and dancing which culminate into a trance or religious ecstasy. So that all people would have access to this religious excitement, Mohammed ordered that mosques be built in the "furthest place," which is what Al Aksa means in Arabic. The Al Aksa can hold at least five thousand worshippers. Men congregate on one side and women on the other. They always pray in the direction of Mecca, the birthplace of Mohammed and the cradle of Islam.

Temple Courtyard Faces Mecca

When Moslems established the shrine, the Dome of the Rock, and then about ten years later the Al Aksa Mosque, the general outline of the ancient Temple Square was followed. However, a shift toward Mecca, more in a southeast direction, is apparent. The major outer courtyards of the ancient temple seem evident even today. Most Moslems are not taught that the ancient temple of Israel ever stood in the same place.

Washings and Anointings

Biblical Font: Between the Dome and the Mosque are several washing areas. One is a washing font that looks similar to one described in the Bible. The biblical font was supported on the backs of twelve oxen.

And he made a molten sea...

The Dome of the Rock on Mount Moriah was built by Caliph Abd-al-Malik in 691 A.D. It is a Moslem shrine commemorating Mohammed's dream of ascending from this rock, as well as Abraham offering his son Ishmael (not Isaac) as a sacrifice.

It stood upon twelve oxen, three looking toward the north, and three looking toward the west, and three looking toward the south, and three looking toward the east: and the sea was set above upon them, and all their hinder parts were inward.   1 KINGS 7:23-25

Moslem Ritual Washings: Moslems symbolically wash themselves in a ritual, starting at their heads, arms, and hands, and ending this washing ceremony at their feet. This is done five times every day before prayers.

Archaeological Discoveries at the Mount

Many people assume that the Dome of the Rock approximates the place of the altar of the ancient temple. The altar of the temple always had to be on bedrock, and the Dome of the Rock is on bedrock. The Dome does not, however, line up with the Gate Beautiful and the peak of the Mount of Olives as in the tradition of the sacrifice of the red heifer.

Possible Location of Holy of Holies: Recent archaeological discoveries by Dr. Asher Kaufman suggest that the Holy of Holies was more to the north of the Dome of the Rock. His studies show it was closer to a small dome, also built on bedrock, which the Arabs call the Dome of the Tablets. This dome does line up with a modern Gate Beautiful and the peak of the Mount of Olives.

The Dome of the Tablets: It is interesting that the Dome of the Tablets also more accurately fits the Jewish tradition that the sacrifice of the red calf on the Mount of Olives had to be in the line of sight of the Gate Beautiful and just north of the altar that was in front of the Holy of Holies. Archaeologist Dr. James Fleming describes the remains of an ancient gate under what many today call Gate Beautiful.

An Ancient Gate Underneath a Grave: Dr. Fleming discovered the remains of an ancient gate beneath the present gate when, as he was standing directly in front of the sealed gate to photograph it, he fell through a grave. I recall Jim Fleming telling us about his tumble into the mass grave. He said he was "frightened to death," but somehow managed to "compose himself." His sense of humor served him well. His curiosity revealed the truth of the statement "What one sees today may be a likeness of what was there before."

Troubled History of the Gate Beautiful: At the end of a large grave room, Dr. Fleming found that the wall directly underneath today's Gate Beautiful once had been a gate itself. It had been filled in as a foundation for the newer gate now standing above. History tells us that after the second temple (Herodian) was destroyed, the Byzantines (third to fourth centuries) rebuilt the Gate Beautiful. Later, the Arabs destroyed it in the seventh century. The Crusaders (twelfth to thirteenth centuries) rebuilt it when they arrived, but the Turks (sixteenth to nineteenth centuries) sealed it up. They placed grave sites directly in front of it. These, they thought, would dissuade the Messiah (a priest is not allowed to walk where the dead are laid) from entering the temple area.

Arabs symbolically wash themselves five times every day just before prayers. They begin with their heads, then wash their arms and hands, and conclude by washing their feet.

Jesus to Enter Through This Gate: Christians, of course, recall the accounts of Jesus raising the dead and appearing to his apostles in a closed room. The Turkish barriers then would not be difficult to overcome when Jesus returns to fulfill the tradition that the Messiah would come through the same entrance again.

Ancient Signs and Tokens: It is fascinating to consider the many legends, stories, prophecies, and numerous details in ancient scriptures that deal with covenants, signs, and tokens. Somehow, they weave patterns of expectation of a first and/or second coming of the Messiah.

We have examined a few patterns that deal with places located just a few hundred yards apart. In this section, we've considered Mount Moriah, the place where Abraham was instructed to bring his son as a sacrificial offering. It is where many suggest the Son of God sacrificed His life—north of the altar. We've considered the Mount of Olives, the place where the ancient and rare sacrifices of a red calf suggested the events at Gethsemane in the meridian of time. It also points to the Messiah's red-clothed advent still to come.

The parallels we have drawn may be unbelievable to some, and they may even be stumbling blocks to them. However, for those who can believe, these parallels and patterns become stepping stones to a spiritual oasis in the Holy Land.

Chapter 14

Ethnic Quarters of the City

Christian Church of the Holy Sepulcher

 The Church of the Holy Sepulcher, located in the Christian Quarter, marks the oldest Christian traditional site of the crucifixion and burial of Jesus. To date, however, different Christian denominations still argue over the control of this church building complex. It was first established three hundred years after the crucifixion of Jesus. The competitive religions include Armenian, Catholic, Coptic, Greek Orthodox, and Syrian Orthodox.

"What one sees today is very often a reflection of what was there before."

Temporary Ethnic Use: The various churches take turns using some of the religious relics, such as the Place of the Cross, the Rock of Unction, or the Sepulcher itself. Various religious clerics are careful not to contend at specific meeting points, although history reveals great arguments over use and ownership rights. To solve these clashes, the priests in turn bring their own carpets, wall hangings, and lamps, as well as different colors and styles of worship vestments. As soon as their worship shift for using a site is over, they remove their things and their temporary ownership ends.

Holy Sepulcher Damage and Repairs: The buildings and edifices in the Holy Sepulcher complex are almost pinched together as a result of centuries of construction. That did not prevent them from being severely damaged by an earthquake in 1927. However, repair work was stymied due to the conflicts of ownership claims. As soon as one church group started repairs, another would stop them, claiming ownership. As a repair might imply possession (and thereby ownership), there was always someone to object. Since the reuniting of Jerusalem with a combined Jewish and Arab influence and authority, the rebuilding of the Church of the Holy Sepulcher has finally been carried out. Replicas have replaced previously shattered pillars and structures, which under British rule had been crudely bound with metal bands since 1927.

Relics of Religion: Some of the relics relating to religious tradition include the "hill" of Calvary (there is no hill mentioned in the New Testament account). There are two highly decorated chambers (small chapels) built where two of the three crosses were supposed to have been. The center of three little archway chapels is built over the place where Jesus' crucifixion purportedly occurred. Another one

signifies the repentant prisoner crucified at the same time. The other chapel, undecorated, probably refers to the prisoner who disparaged Jesus. Although the New Testament translations refer to the prisoners as thieves, research shows that according to Jewish and Roman law, there was nothing worth stealing that was punishable by crucifixion. The prisoners crucified with Jesus were probably sentenced to die for treason or murder.

Rock of Unction: Close by and at the foot of the "rock" of crucifixion is the Rock of Unction, where tradition says the body was prepared and anointed for burial. This traditional Jewish ritual includes immersing and washing the body and then anointing it with highly spiced oils. Christians have venerated the Rock of Unction as the slab on which this preparation was made.

The Sepulcher: Quite close is a structure (the fourth one rebuilt at this spot), said to be the sepulcher of Jesus. There are two chambers that represent a weeping or mourning chamber and the burial room. In the second room a slab of marble is shown as the place of Jesus' final earthly resting place. Since there is no marble indigenous to Israel, the slab was probably brought from elsewhere and not likely used in any original, first-century Jewish burial.

Tombs for Joseph of Arimathaea: Some nearby tombs are also exhibited as the final resting spot for Joseph of Arimathaea who according to the scriptures, had given his own tomb for Jesus. It is said that the small chapel at this area is claimed by the Armenian Church; but the Syrian Orthodox Church still meets there, refusing to give up its rights. The standoff is evident, as the Armenians do not allow Syrian Church members to decorate or repair this alcove (which would imply ownership).

Commemorative Chapels for St. Helena: Other chapels are commemorative of St. Helena. According to tradition, St. Helena identified the relic of the true cross in Jerusalem and identified the location of the Holy Sepulcher. She suggested that "digging would reveal the wood of the cross upon which Jesus hung." Various pieces of wood have been brought forth throughout the centuries, prompting one artist to paint "the tree" from which the cross was made. The painting shows branches of various species, as there are pieces of different kinds of wood. Another nearby chapel is built on the place where a sword or spear, possibly the one that pierced Jesus, was found. Crusaders searched for the sword that pierced Jesus, thinking that would lead them to victory over the Moslems. Another venerated spot is the supposed burial site of Adam and Eve. That is conveniently located directly underneath the spot where Jesus was said to have been crucified. Some suggest that the "first blood" of atonement flowed through the rock, seeping down below, to redeem the "first sinners."

Disputes for Religious Rights: As previously stated, these are sites that have been the focus of Christian worship for many centuries. Moslems would conquer, then Christians would reconquer. At present there is peace, but the keys of the Holy Sepulcher are still in the hands of a Moslem. Actually, this eliminates domination of one church over the other. The Christian section of Jerusalem is directly next to the Moslem section. Although they have been battling each other for centuries, a fairly quiet coexistence has been reached this century. Nevertheless, property rights and

"Holy Sepulcher," fourth structure built since Byzantine times.

During Palm Sunday, many Christians throng the Holy City to visit the Church of the Holy Sepulcher, the traditional site of the burial of Jesus. However, others believe that the real site is located outside the wall of the city in a garden.

ownership questions are constantly surfacing. That is probably exacerbated by the return of Jews to the Old City. They are insisting on previous ownership rights that may have been taken over by Moslems or Christians since 1948. In other situations, the Jews are purchasing property from owners whose previous landlords prohibited subsequent sale to Jews. Underlying the legal disputes are the religious "rights" or at least religious feelings that have continued on for centuries.

Moslem Section

The Arab Suk (Market): The "real life" of grocery shopping is patterned after the market practices followed for centuries. In butcher shops, the consumable animal parts are cleanly displayed. Situated alongside in another shop could be tinsmiths, banging on their anvils and forming items such as little coal stoves to cook the meat. Every day you can see the broom maker assembling straw bristles without handles, as he stacks or hangs them neatly in rows by sizes. Nearby, vegetable and fruit produce is laid neatly side by side as if the display were an art form. Shops with brightly-embroidered dresses line the alcove-covered streets. The dresses often show the genealogy of the original owner, who probably made them herself. Spice and herb displays add to the sheer color and fragrance of the *suk*, the market. They create a festival of sights, sounds, and smells never to be forgotten.

Jewish Quarter

From Ruins to Rebuilding: From 1948 to 1967, the Jewish Quarter lacked Jewish residents. In the 1948 War of Independence, this quarter was besieged and every synagogue in the quarter was destroyed. Jews eventually surrendered, and the quarter became a slum. In 1966, King Hussein of Jordan ordered Arab squatters out of the rundown area. By 1967 the entire courtyard leading to the Western or Wailing Wall was still filled with hovels and the ruins of the old Jerusalem Jewish Quarter. Then the courtyard was cleared as the Jewish Quarter came back into Jewish hands. The Old City was again reunited with the rest of Jerusalem; excavations were carried out, and new residences were tastefully built in and around the ruins dating back twenty-seven hundred years.

Herodian Excavations: The upper part of the city, where many of the priestly class lived during the first century, has been excavated, revealing the fire destruction at the time Titus destroyed the city in 70 A.D. Immense cisterns have been discovered, as well as immersion baths that had separate water storage. Jewish mikvahs could then be done with "pure" or "living" water, as required by Jewish ritual law. The opulence and class of this part of the city are revealed by comparing written accounts and the archaeological discoveries of modern times.

The Burnt House, an Ancient Jewish Home: A home discovered in the excavations of the Jewish Quarter belonged to a Kathros family. The ruins reveal priestly functions and ritual items. The Kathros name is known in Jewish writings as one of the corrupt priestly families of the first century. Remains of the home have been left intact, and a special multi-image film presentation explains the

Orthodox Jews walking up the Mount of Olives to pray.

excavation of the Jewish Quarter. The displays present cups and dishes made of stone (very kosher). There is a stone mold that was a money-making facility. One can clearly connect this to the scriptural account of money changers. The archaeological explanation for nails on display is that they were used in furniture or house construction. However, we know that nails were also used in ritual ways. More details about worship practices are given in Chapter 16.

The Cardo, Ancient Shopping Malls: The shopping malls today are built like they were in times past. Archways are still in use for many of the shops lining the street, reminding us of how they looked anciently. The malls and streets today are almost directly above ancient streets and malls. Excavations reveal parts of streets, drainage channels, foundations for homes and stores, and even some complete shops that have remained intact. The shop alcoves had lofts for storage or the midafternoon nap. One remaining shop had a deep niche in one corner. I can just imagine the walls covered with goods on display, and behind is a nook for extra inventory. Maybe it was to hide merchandise from the ever-snooping tax man! It is interesting how similar the mode of life is today and even how similar the structures and streets are as in ancient times. What one sees today is very often a reflection of what was there before.

*A Jewish Sukkot market in Mea Shearim,
the Orthodox Jewish section of Jerusalem.
Many Biblical traditions and holy days are
commemorated in similar ways in Israel
today. It is still a land of sacred duty.*

SCRIPTURAL REFERENCES (KJV)

Section Four

Features of Today's Jerusalem

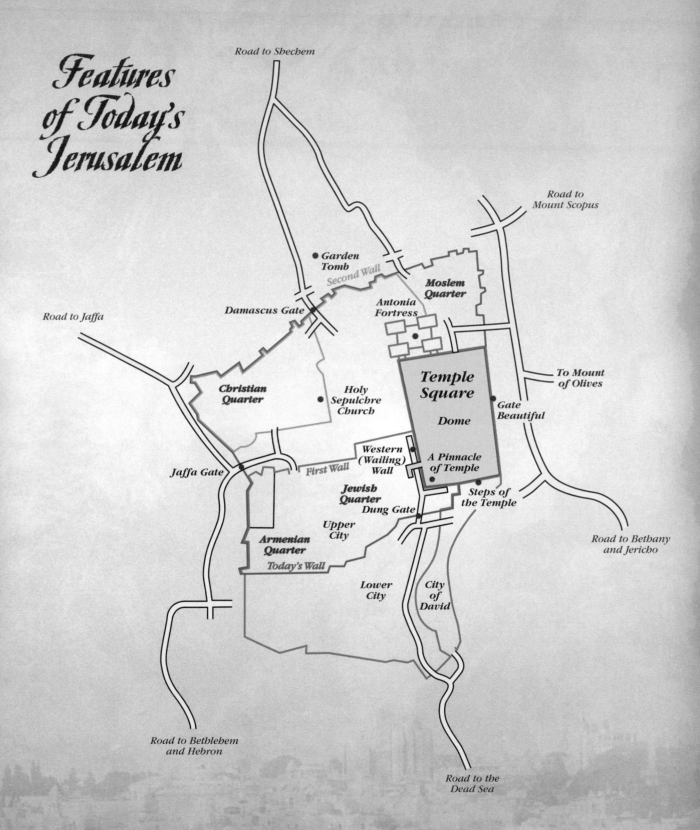

Road to Shechem

Road to Mount Scopus

Garden Tomb

Second Wall

Moslem Quarter

Damascus Gate

Antonia Fortress

Road to Jaffa

Christian Quarter

Holy Sepulchre Church

Temple Square

Dome

To Mount of Olives

Gate Beautiful

Western (Wailing) Wall

A Pinnacle of Temple

First Wall

Jaffa Gate

Jewish Quarter

Dung Gate

Steps of the Temple

Upper City

Road to Bethany and Jericho

Armenian Quarter

Today's Wall

Lower City

City of David

Road to Bethlehem and Hebron

Road to the Dead Sea

- Overview -
Jerusalem at Worship

In **JERUSALEM**, the old and new **CITY GATES** bring you into the streets of the **ARAB BAZAAR**. They are an interesting contrast to the **JEWISH CARDO**, another ancient **MALL**. Examining the ancient **JEWISH QUARTER** and the **WOHL HERODIAN** living center, a residential **"CONDOMINIUM"** that was found underneath today's city, provides an exciting connection of the "old" and the "new" Jerusalem. The **ISRAEL MUSEUM** displays many artifacts that deal directly with biblical accounts and worship practices. You can find artifacts of **TEMPLE SITES** and **ALTARS**. There are cave inscriptions from the so-called **LEHI CAVE** dating to 600 B.C. that are similar to the Book of Mormon account of Jews fleeing Jerusalem. A view of the **DEAD SEA SCROLLS** and a closer examination of the doctrines and covenants of the **ESSENES** is exciting. Their organization and system of vows are comparable to ancient Judaism and provide Latter-day Saints with a comparison to their own modern religious organization and doctrine. Some of the **OLDEST BIBLICAL TEXTS** are revealed in the writings of the Dead Sea Scrolls.

Jerusalem's Old City eastern wall awakens in the early morning sunshine as the valley below is still asleep in darkness.

Chapter 15

Jerusalem's Gates

There is no other city quite like Jerusalem. Once you have visited her, you cannot forget her. To me, Jerusalem is the jewel in God's crown—and the crown of Jerusalem was, is, and will be her temple. The temple is God's house on the earth, and it contains the sacred secrets of what was, what is, and what will be. Let's discover this city of worshiping, a habitat of holy places, doorways, and gates that lead to the traditions and memories that have extended throughout the ages. So powerful is its importance that one of the Psalms says,

> *If I forget thee, O Jerusalem, let my right hand forget her cunning.*
> *PSALM 137:5*

Northern Gates of Jerusalem

New Gate: This is the newest gate in the walls of Jerusalem leading to the Christian Quarter. It was built in the 1800s, but was closed between 1948 and 1967, as Arabs had taken over all of Jerusalem. In 1967, Israel opened the gate again, and Israeli soldiers helped nuns leave the Christian confines through this gate. They led them to the safety of the Notre Dame Catholic Hospice across the street.

Although the New Gate is a convenient entrance to the Christian Quarter, a small Moslem mosque stands at the entrance. Its Muezzin's loud speakers ring out in high decibels as a reminder that Islam has made its presence known. Sprinkled throughout the Christian Quarter are other mosques, daily broadcasting their five calls to prayer.

Damascus Gate: This is the largest and most impressive of all the gates. It is called *Sha'ar Shechem* (Shechem Gate) in Hebrew and *Bab El Amud* (Gate of the Pillar) in Arabic. Hadrian's statue stood on a pillar just inside the gate in the second century. Remains of a first-century Roman gate have recently been uncovered. In addition to the first and second-century ruins, there are Crusader remains to be seen as well. At a level two stories below today's twentieth-century street, people still enter the city through the gate built in 1538 by the Turkish Sultan, Suleiman the Magnificent. Recently, as remains of the first and second-century gate were found about two stories below the present gate, a small "hands-on" museum with ancient artifacts was opened.

An Olive Press: In recent history, one of the names given to the gate or street is *Zay'et* (olives). It has had a connotation of olives or olive pressing. During the

"Once annually, a firstborn, unblemished animal was allowed to escape out this gate after it had been 'blessed' with the sins of the congregation."

recent excavations the reason for this name was discovered, as a giant olive press and storage facility were uncovered. Apparently, pressing olives in the hills or fields became a liability because thieves would steal the oil. Bringing the olives to the city to be turned into oil had the advantage of protection by the massive walls and plenty of population.

Herod's Gate: This gate was named by medieval pilgrims because of the close proximity of the "Antonia Fortress" which Herod built. Remains of Herod's second wall, where Herod's Gate stands, may also add to the tradition of its name. In Hebrew, it is called *Sha'ar HaPrachim* (Gate of Flowers) because of the floral designs in the stonework. This is the most convenient entrance to the Moslem Quarter of the old city.

Fruit Vendors Inside the Gate: Fruit vendors crowd the entrance. Just inside are little family shops. Their sales are specialized in particular goods. For example, the "nut man" has been there for generations. His display of nuts is typical, but his speciality is in preparing fresh, dried, and roasted pistachios. They are unmatched anywhere in Jerusalem. The fragrance greets you as you enter Herod's Gate.

Eastern Gates from the Kidron Valley

Lions' Gate: Lions adorning the walls on each side of the gate are symbols of the Egyptian Sultan Baybars I. With his troops, he wrought heavy destruction on the Crusaders in the thirteenth century. The gate itself was built in 1538 by Sultan Suleiman the Magnificent. There is an incorrect tradition that Stephen was stoned at this location; therefore, it has been given the incorrect name of Saint Stephen's Gate. It is extremely unlikely that Jewish stonings would be allowed this close to the temple, as there is no Jewish precedent for it. The temple was for the "noble or honorable" deaths or sacrifices. Stonings were done outside the city walls—where criminals were thrown from a cliff, as described in a previous chapter. In 1967, the Israeli military entered the city from this gate. Historically, this had happened only once before when Judas the Macabee conquered the Greek/Syrian government in the year 164 B.C. Usually, the high Mount of Olives and the steep Kidron Valley below made this approach a most unlikely spot to enter the city. Obviously, an approaching enemy would be seen from the walls of the city, and the gate would be secured.

Golden Gate (Gate Beautiful): This is the most significant gate of the Temple. It is also known as the "Gate of Mercy" and the "Gate of Forgiveness," *Sha'ar HaRahamim* in Hebrew. Located close to the middle of the temple's eastern wall, it was built to be just north of the altar.

Gate Used by the Scapegoat: Once annually, a firstborn, unblemished animal was allowed to escape out this gate after it had been "blessed" with the sins of the congregation. This lamb or goat symbolically carried the sins of the congregation. That animal, the scapegoat, was marked with a red ribbon and escaped death at the north side of the altar. Jewish tradition says that the ribbon was to remind all that the marked animal could not be killed but was to meet death on its own outside the temple.

An interior view of the Golden Gate reveals that it is now a room with a door instead of a passageway. This room holds chairs and tables, and is supported by ancient pillars which may have come from Herod's temple compound.

Messiah Entered Through This Gate: In the meridian of time, the Messiah entered this gate, and took the sins of all people on himself, the true and eternal sacrifice. He was not killed. He died on his own.

> *...Father, into thy hands I commend my spirit: and having said thus, he gave up the ghost.* LUKE 23:46

This occurred outside the temple, north of the altar at the Place of a Skull.

Gate Sealed by the Turks: As mentioned in Chapter 13, in the sixteenth century Turks sealed the Gate Beautiful and placed a Moslem graveyard in front of it to dissuade the Jewish or Christian Messiah from entering. (The Messiah was considered to be a priest—and priests could have no contact or proximity with the dead except in sacrifices.)

Southern Gates

Dung Gate: The Dung Gate is located on the south side of today's city walls. In Byzantine times, there was a small gate close by. It was rediscovered by excavations since 1967. Until recent centuries, the sewage and waste of the city was also channeled through this gate. That is probably how it became known as the Dung Gate. In 1948, the Jordanians attacked the city through this gate, destroying much of it as they widened it. They brought military equipment into the city to besiege the Jewish Quarter. The present gate has been reconstructed and kept wide to handle modern traffic. It is the nearest gate to the Western (Wailing) Wall. Vendors with portable stands greet you with freshly baked rings of Arab bread, generously sprinkled with toasted sesame seeds. Just inside the gate, various "charity takers" are giving passersby the opportunity of giving to the poor. Some of them give red threads for you to wear as a sign of your generosity. Possibly, this is some symbolic link to the red ribbon tied around the scapegoat that was led out of the eastern gate of the temple.

Zion Gate: The Zion Gate is also located on the southwestern side of the city. This bullet-scarred gate was the scene of fierce fighting in 1948 as the Arabs battled to capture the Jewish Quarter. This ethnic neighborhood had been inhabited by Jews for close to a thousand years. Although the Palmach (a unit of underground commandos breaking up the Arab siege of Jerusalem) breached it in 1948, the population in the Jewish Quarter eventually surrendered anyway. The name Zion's Gate comes from the incorrect tradition that it is on Mount Zion and close to the City of David. Both Mount Zion and the City of David have been archaeologically and biblically identified directly south of the Temple Mount, not westward where this gate is.

Western Gate

Jaffa Gate: The Jaffa Gate is often considered the busiest gate of Jerusalem. It was built by Sultan Suleiman the Magnificent in the 1500s. In 1898, the German Kaiser, Wilhelm II, could not get his entourage of horses, wagons, and decorated coaches

A Greek holy man walks the streets of Old Jerusalem. The streets are closed to cars and trucks during the shopping hours of the day. Many streets are too narrow for any vehicles except small two wheeled carts.

through the gate. As with most gates, a sharp left turn was required. This turn was a way to slow intruders in case of an enemy attack that might have broken through the fortified doors. So the wall of the city next to the gate was broken open. The German Kaiser's convoy was then able to enter the city directly. Tradition suggests that the stones removed from the wall were reused to build a German Lutheran Church close to the Holy Sepulcher.

General Allenby: British General Edmund Allenby also used this Jaffa Gate entrance when he accepted the surrender of the Turks. The Turks, incidentally, had to "surrender" a few times, because each subsequent officer felt more empowered than his underling to accept the capitulation.

The Gate's Loopholes: Jaffa Gate, restored by the Israelis since 1967, still contains the typical oil chutes and loopholes used to defend the city and gate during Turkish times. Loopholes are slits in the very thick wall that broaden out toward the inside so that a soldier has enough maneuvering space to shoot out. The slit on the outside allows little chance of return fire entering the loophole. Invariably, any lawyer on tour wants his picture taken by these slits. Conjecture says the term loophole derived its legal meaning from the same concept—namely, a lot of angle on one side and very little on the other.

A young Jewish boy becomes Bar Mitzvah during this celebration at the Western Wall in Jerusalem.

Chapter 16

Moslem and Jewish Rites

Templc Square

 Mount Moriah and the Temple: Mount Moriah must be examined more than just casually to discover the reason it was designated for the temple. In that same location is the third-holiest site of the Moslems in this area of the world, the Dome of the Rock. We can learn about Moslems preparing for worship at the nearby Al Aksa Mosque. On a level below these sites, along the Western Wall of what was once Temple Square, we can observe the religious practices of Jews at the so-called Wailing Wall.

Islam and Mohammed

Worship Practices of Moslems: Understanding the worship and the practices of the Moslems can help us appreciate the design and beauty of the Islamic Center on Mount Moriah. Islam was started about six hundred years after Jesus' time by Mohammed. He saw both Christianity and Judaism as apostate religions. They contained only part of the truths he felt he had received from the angel Gabriel during his historic "Night Vision." In this dream or vision, while in Arabia, Mohammed was transported from the "rock" (now under the Dome of the Rock), on a steed, *Burak*, into various heavens. The religion of Islam incorporates various tenets, stories, and doctrines of both Judaism and Christianity. *Islam* is the name of the religion, and *Moslem* means "a follower of Islam."

The Koran: It is a clearly stated instruction in the Koran that people of the "Book," the Bible, meaning Jews and Christians, are to be protected and valued as friends of the Moslems. The Koran is a collection of the sayings of Mohammed as he was instructed by the angel Gabriel. These things were written down by various scribes. It is said that Mohammed himself was not able to read or write. However, that seems less likely if the account of his being a merchant is correct.

Dervishes and Flying Carpets: Mohammed's own religious experiences were charismatic and remarkable. Because he was able to repeat them again and again and reach a consistent level of religious excitement, he instructed people to become Dervishes and to form schools to teach others to experience this new exhilaration. (*Dervishes* are known as people able to bring themselves into a high charismatic religious trance, even to the point of not feeling pain as they pierce

---

"*The imagery or pattern of ancient temple practices can still be seen as people congregate for traditional worship below the Temple Square along the Western Wall.*"

themselves with hooks or knives.) The ecstasy of this group worship was enhanced with great worship halls that contained highly decorated motifs on the walls, windows, and ceilings. A carpet was used to separate the worshiper from the earth. It is assumed that due to the euphoria of worship on these carpets, the term flying carpets came to be known. Now, you know! It isn't the carpet that is flying.   The worshiper is in a religious "high flight" of feeling. To keep distraction at a minimum, worshiping men and women were also separated into segregated sections.   These special meeting halls are now known as *mosques*. Due to the diversity of the Moslem population, many political leaders have used the mosque as a platform for their ideologies. The euphoria of these political quests is thusly connected to the religious environment and many followers accept the political concepts as religious doctrine.

Five Pillars of Islam: The Five Pillars of Islam (basic tenants or beliefs) include:

(1) Worshiping of Allah (Allah is a "singular/neutral" word, the Arabic way of pronouncing *Elohim*. Elohim in Hebrew is a "plural/masculine" word);

(2) Praying five times a day in the direction of Mecca, preceded by ritual washing each time;

(3) Paying tithes and offerings for the poor;

(4) Fasting for a monthly period every year during the daytime (*Ramadan*); and

(5) Going to Mecca once in a lifetime. Along with the washings at Mecca and the wearing of white robe-like clothing, Moslems are given a "new name," one that they must not reveal—for it is theirs to use in the next life when they approach Allah.

The Importance of Mecca: It is interesting that Moslems are urged to return to Mecca again and again, but these pilgrimages are for or in behalf of other people, preferably relatives, who did not have the chance to go. Apparently, they may get the "new name" for them as well. Mecca is the holiest spot for Moslems; it is where Mohammed was born. Close to Mecca is Medina, the second-holiest site for Moslems because it is the place where Mohammed was buried.

The Al Aksa Mosque: The Al Aksa Mosque in Jerusalem was built in the year 701 A.D.; it has undergone at least four major renovations since then.   Moslem authorities in Jerusalem are quite concerned about any kind of diggings around or under their complex. However, they have made their own non-archaeological excavation underneath the mosque which have revealed remains of ancient corridors used by the money changers and vendors of sacrificial animals in the days of Herod's temple. The last Al Aksa remodeling was undertaken after a disturbed Australian tourist set fire to the mosque in 1969. A major remodeling is currently in progress underneath the mosque.

Remnants of Solomon's Temple: Discoveries of burnt embers of cedar wood removed in this repair suggest that parts of the ancient temple may have somehow been re-used in the past to build the mosque. I have seen large cedar timbers in storage under the building. The original Temple of Solomon had cedar beams transported from Lebanon. It is appealing to think that some of the cedar timbers still in existence may be leftovers of almost three thousand years ago.

An Arab reads the Koran inside the Al Aksa Mosque on the temple mount in Jerusalem. The multi-colored rugs and inlaid tiles of the mosque provide a glorious atmosphere for religious meditation.

*This small dome is thought to mark the site of
the north end of the altar close to the Holy of
Holies in the ancient Israelite temple. Other
temple ruins may lie close by underground.
But archaeological digs are not allowed
on the Temple Mount.*

> *And the great court round about was with three rows of hewed*
> *stones, and a row of cedar beams, both for the inner court of the*
> *house of the Lord, and for the porch of the house.*   *1 KINGS 7:12*

Mosques are built and designed for group worship. The Al Aksa Mosque was built ten years after the Dome of the Rock was constructed.

Dome of the Rock: The Dome of the Rock, as mentioned previously in Chapter 13, is the third-holiest site for Moslems. It was built in 691 A.D. and recovered with a 24-karat gold dome in 1994. The Dome of the Rock, unlike mosques that are always directed toward Mecca, has eight walls that symbolically face out into every direction. It is suggested that instead of pointing toward Mecca, like a mosque does, the highly decorated Dome of the Rock draws attention to heaven. This building may have been inspired by a major split in Islam after Mohammed's death. One group continued to worship at or toward Mecca; the other group waited for the prophet Mohammed's replacement and worshiped Allah directly.

The Dome of the Tablets

There are numerous domes and cupolas on the Temple Mount, most of which are named after a great teacher, leader, or *Imam*. The followers and family of these Imams, or other prominent leaders, congregated at these spots to worship. One dome, however, is not named after a man. This dome is built over a small section of Mount Moriah's bedrock and is called the "Dome of the Tablets." Another Arab tradition calls it the "Dome of the Spirit."

Possible Location of the Holy of Holies: Recent archaeological studies indicate that it may be here that the altar of Holy of Holies of the ancient Israelite temple stood. In other words, the Dome of the Tablets is more likely closer to the innermost and holiest part of the temple than the Dome of the Rock.

Urim and Thummim: Among other things, the original Holy of Holies contained the tablets of Mount Sinai and the Urim and Thummim, spiritual tools of discernment. It is tempting to connect the Arab traditional name of the Dome of the Spirit with the location of the "spirit tools" of the Urim and Thummim. These ideas were suggested by Dr. Asher Kaufman, a religious Jew with credible insight concerning archaeological and religious possibilities.

Wilson's Arch

Anciently, exiting Temple Square to the west, one would have descended into a north-south ravine, the Tyropeon Valley. Today it is filled with rubble from the destroyed Jewish temple that stood above on the east side of the valley. It is also filled with the rubble from the ancient ruined city that stretched upward on the west side of the valley.

Archaeology Excavations: The latest excavations reveal the remains of the very bridge that led from Herod's palace to the temple itself and the only known-to-date remains of the western wall that supported Temple Square. The bridge crossed the Tyropeon Valley. Today, some of this excavation is known as Wilson's Arch.

Present-Day Use: In modern times, the bridge archways conveniently house a worship area for Jews wishing to be as close to the Holy of Holies as possible. Various "arks" containing Torah scrolls are also kept here. Three times a week, entourages of male worshippers come into these chambers to collect the scrolls for the Bar Mitzvah or Sabbath readings. Due to recent excavations, there are a number of tunnels leading to this area. On rainy days, when the regular Western (Wailing) Wall is not suitable, women worshippers are allowed to use the tunnels to congregate in Wilson's Arch to view the Bar Mitzvah celebrations. Excavations are now open for small groups to walk along the Western Wall to its north end.

Western (Wailing) Wall

A Substitute for Ancient Temple Worship: This wall is the most significant worship area for religious Jews. The wall itself is not holy. However, since Orthodox Jews feel they cannot go on the Temple Mount because the priesthood was considered lost after the temple was destroyed in the year 70 A.D., this wall serves as the closest reminder. The imagery or pattern of ancient temple practices can still be seen as people congregate for traditional worship below the Temple Square along the Western Wall. Religious Jews have gathered here for centuries; their activities are reminders of what might have occurred in the Temple anciently and are recognizable to LDS temple visitors today.

Temple Symbolism

Special Clothing Worn: Traditions that still occur include men worshiping separately from women. Men wear special clothing, such as a head covering called a *kipa* in Hebrew, or *yarmulke* in Yiddish. Women also cover their hair and some even wear veils. Sometimes, male Levites wear an apron, and others wear a sash tied on one side. The ever-present prayer shawl or robe is draped over the shoulders (first it is draped over one shoulder and then over the other). The prayer shawl is usually made of wool and is called a *talith* (a word derived from the Hebrew word *taleh*, which is "wool from a lamb"). Clothing in addition to the talith can sometimes be seen worn on one shoulder or the other as well. Older Jews remind us that, in times past, they removed their shoes because the site was so holy.

Nail in a Sure Place: I discovered an even older custom when I realized that hundreds, if not thousands, of nails were pounded into the Western Wall. Older texts reveal a now-forgotten custom of the "sure nails." This was the practice of bringing one's sins, grief, or the tragedies of life to the remains of the temple wall and "nailing" them in a sure place. The nails are a reminder of Isaiah's prophecy that man's burden will be removed when the nail in the sure place is taken down.

These arches are part of an ancient
bridge that led from Herod's palace to the
temple. Now it is a worship area for Jews
who want to be as close as possible to the
Holy of Holies that once stood near here.

An Orthodox Jew prays on a bench at the Western Wall while others rush by on their way home. Devout Jews come to this wall from all over the world to pray and praise God.

> *In that day, saith the Lord of hosts, shall the nail that is fastened in the sure place be removed, and be cut down, and fall; and the burden that was upon it shall be cut off: for the Lord hath spoken it.   ISAIAH 22:25*

Phylacteries: There are other practices, such as phylacteries that are wrapped around the arm and hand, and on the head. These customs follow a precise procedure and words of prayer. There always seems to be someone on hand to assist and prompt the worshiper to wrap the phylacteries correctly. This practice follows the Biblical commandment to "bind the Lord's word to the heart and head."

> *Hear, O Israel: the LORD our God is one LORD:*
>
> *And thou shalt love the LORD thy God with all thine heart, and with all thy soul, and with all thy might.*
>
> *And these words, which I comand thee this day, shall be in thine heart:*
>
> *And thou shalt teach them diligently unto thy children, and shalt talk of them when thou sittest in thine house, and when thou walkest by the way, and when thou liest down, and when thou risest up.*
>
> *And thou shalt bind them for a sign upon thine hand, and they shall be as frontlets between thine eyes.*
>
> *And thou shalt write them upon the posts of thy house, and on thy gates.   DEUTERONOMY 6:4-9*

A similar commandment was given in the modern times, as the Lord revealed instructions for keeping the Lord's word and spirit in our incomings and outgoings.

> *And that this house may be a house of prayer, a house of fasting, a house of faith, a house of glory and of God, even thy house;*
>
> *That all the incomings of thy people, into this house, may be in the name of the Lord;*
>
> *That all their outgoings from this house may be in the name of the Lord;*
>
> *And that all their salutations may be in the name of the Lord, with holy hands, uplifted to the Most High;*
> *DOCTRINE & COVENANTS 109:16-19*

Prayer Lists: The bits of paper stuck in the cracks of this ancient Herodian wall, for the most part, are thought of as prayers. In that sense, it has become kind of a "wishing wall." More secular Jews have resorted to writing prayers or wishes on bits of paper and stuffing them into the cracks of the wall. A recent worldly approach to making prayers more convenient is to send them to a fax machine or e-mail close by! Someone will place them into the wall for you. However, the older orthodox practice is still to place lists of names of those needing special prayers. I suppose the symbolism is that the worshippers invoke God's blessing for those whose names are presented. The service is performed for those in need by those presenting the names.

Archaeology Reveals Ancient Customs: People standing at the bottom of the Western Wall are dwarfed by the immense size of the Herodian blocks and the sheer height of the wall.   Yet, the original base of this wall is another sixty feet below where people gather today.   This is a typical example of how the Old City of Jerusalem is layered upon itself after many destructions and reconstructions. Archaeological examinations of about two dozen layers show how the city has continued to exist throughout thousands of years. Examination of religious practices also shows how traditions have continued to exist, revealing an insight to sacred temple customs of the past.

Mount Moriah and the Jebusites

King David at Moriah: Over three millennia ago, the hill Moriah, which was later known as Jerusalem, was controlled by Jebusites when King David came to conquer them in the name of the Lord. The city was strongly fortified with steep canyons or ravines (the Kidron on the east and the Tyropeon on the west) and high walls that towered above them. David's army stood hundreds of feet below while the Jebusites jeered them from above. The Jebusites taunted David's army by saying that if they, the inhabiters, were sick and lame, David's army could not conquer them.

> *And the king and his men went to Jerusalem unto the Jebusites,*
> *the inhabitants of the land: which spake unto David, saying,*
> *Except thou take away the blind and the lame, thou shalt not*
> *come in hither: thinking, David cannot come in hither.*
> *2 SAMUEL 5:6*

David Conquers the Jebusites: David quickly perceived that the Jebusite drinking water came from just outside their eastern city wall. The Gihon Spring in the Kidron Valley below had been diverted by the Jebusites through a short tunnel under the wall. A shaft was then used to draw the water up into their stronghold. The Bible relates how David's nephew, Joab, swam through the flooded tunnel, climbed up the shaft at night, and unlocked the Jebusite gates. That opened the way for David's army to conquer without force. The tunnel and shaft continued to be used to provide drinking water for this City of David for another three hundred years. However, it also remained a weak spot in the city's defense perimeter.

Hezekiah's Tunnel

The Pool of Siloam: It was Hezekiah who lengthened the tunnel to the other side of the City of David, diverting the continuously flowing spring to a very large pool named the Pool of Siloam.

*Hezekiah's Tunnel emerges from solid rock
and empties water from the Gihon Spring
into the Pool of Siloam. It was here that
Jesus sent the blind man to wash in the
living water and be healed.*

> *This same Hezekiah also stopped the upper watercourse of Gihon,*
> *and brought it straight down to the west side of the city of David.*
> *And Hezekiah prospered in all his works.   2 CHRONICLES 32:30*

The pool was in what is now called the Tyropeon Valley, and it was still within the now-expanded city walls. The Gihon Spring was then totally covered, and thereby that access to the city was concealed.

Lengthening the Tunnel: To create the lengthened tunnel, two teams worked from opposite ends, chipping and cutting toward each other, following the softer veins in the stone.   Turning and correcting themselves, they finally met less than two feet apart, having carved a tunnel through almost eighteen hundred feet of stone. The Gihon Spring end of the tunnel is eighteen inches higher than the Siloam Pool end, so that the water could flow easily. Some of the original plaster still remains. In modern times, the tunnel was cleared so that fresh spring water and adventurous visitors could pass through.

Jesus at the Pool of Siloam: Twenty-seven hundred years ago, Hezekiah's Tunnel was (and still is) a wonder of human ingenuity. Seven hundred years later, Jesus caused another wonder that irritated the Jewish priests at this same place. A little background makes the account even more meaningful. It is important to know that Jesus was referred to as the "Fountain of Living Waters" before he came to earth. Living waters would heal and save.

> *O Lord, the hope of Israel, all that forsake thee shall be ashamed, and*
> *they that depart from me shall be written in the earth, because they*
> *have forsaken the Lord, the fountain of living waters.*
>
> *Heal me, O Lord, and I shall be healed; save me, and I shall be saved:*
> *for thou art my praise.   JEREMIAH 17:13-14*

The Name Siloam: The name Siloam, *shiloach* in Hebrew, means "sent." The fresh, living waters that flowed through the tunnel were "sent" to the Pool of Siloam. Jesus saved a blind man by "sending" him to the pool of "sent" to receive sight, to see the light. The blind man was healed by washing his eyes in living waters; he was healed by the "Fountain of Living Waters."

Another Name for Jesus: Another name for Jesus is the "Light of the World." He was sent from God to give us sight and light. The Hebrew wording of John's gospel account of this miracle portrays this insightful symbolism.

> *As long as I am in the world, I am the light of the world.*
>
> *When he had thus spoken, he spat on the ground, and made clay*
> *of the spittle, and he anointed the eyes of the blind man with*
> *the clay,*
>
> *And said unto him, Go, wash in the pool of Siloam, (which is by*
> *interpretation, Sent.) He went his way therefore, and washed, and*
> *came seeing.   JOHN 9:5-7*

Chapter 17

Antiquities and Ancient Records

Israel Museum

 Prehistoric Antiquities in Israel: The foremost place to see artifacts of the past is in the Israel Museum. Antiquities dating to a prehistoric time, that include manlike beings, are carefully displayed in chronological order. The existence of this prehistoric being is suggested. The oldest tools of these prehistoric manlike beings are coarse and primarily used for hunting. Later, the tools become finer in workmanship and show learned abilities in agriculture and culture. Beads and decorative wearing apparel also seem to predate civilization. There is a unique archaeological difference with the transition to civilization. Biblically, civilization comes with the first man and woman, Adam and Eve. Their technology includes pottery, whereas prehistoric beings only worked with stone tools and ate with stone vessels.

Biblical Antiquities: Tools and weapons dating from Adam's to Noah's time also show high skills in metal working.

> *And Zillah, she also bare Tubal-cain, an instructor of every artificer in brass and iron: and the sister of Tubal-cain was Naamah.*
> GENESIS 4:22

Many of these tools are very similar to instruments still in use today. For example, saws, woodwork planes, and knives have been found. The knives have wooden handles riveted or pinned onto the metal blades. Decorated pottery and exquisite jewelry date to the time of Abraham and Moses. Since there is no metal found in Israel, ingots were transported from the Sinai Peninsula and Egypt.

Idols and Worship Altars: Numerous idols and worship altars remind us of the challenges the children of Israel faced as they returned from Egypt. Were they going to follow the God of Israel or worship these idols made of stone and wood?

> *I call heaven and earth to witness against you this day, that ye shall soon utterly perish from off the land whereunto ye go over Jordan to possess it; ye shall not prolong your days upon it, but shall utterly be destroyed.*

> *And the Lord shall scatter you among the nations, and ye shall be left few in number among the heathen, whither the Lord shall lead you.*

"Jews still have the custom to 'wear' the name of God as if they are taking his name upon them."

*Arab calligraphy from the Koran dominates
these beautifully designed Persian tiles.*

> *And there ye shall serve gods, the work of men's hands, wood and stone, which neither see, nor hear, nor eat, nor smell.*
>
> *But if from thence thou shalt seek the Lord thy God, thou shalt find him, if thou seek him with all thy heart and with all thy soul.*
> DEUTERONOMY 4:26-29

Worship of the Sun and Moon: One altar found at Tel Hazor depicts two hands upstretched in an attitude of prayer or supplication to a sun and moon. Drawings of the sun, moon, and stars may have had religious meanings in these temples or centers of worship.

> *And lest thou lift up thine eyes unto heaven, and when thou seest the sun, and the moon, and the stars, even all the host of heaven, shouldest be driven to worship them, and serve them, which the Lord thy God hath divided unto all nations under the whole heaven.* DEUTERONOMY 4:19

Cherubim and Angels: Other imagery included cherubim depicted by "animal angels," such as cats or lions guarding the entrance to Temples. Another fascinating artifact was of a winged "human angel" guarding a tree. This was found in the ancient temple site of Hazor.

Wearing the Name of God: Historical accounts on clay, stone, and metal plates or tablets often correspond with biblical accounts. A recent discovery included small gold or silver-like tablets with scripture verses written on them. They were found in a stone box dating back to six hundred years before Jesus' time. The inscription may likely have been the ancient version of the *Shma Israel*, a blessing or main credo of Israelite believers in God. Jews still have the custom to "wear" the name of God as if they are taking his name upon them. Since the name of God is not to be spoken, it has become the custom to wear a description of him. Following is the credo/name that apparently was used at the time these metallic mini-scrolls were made.

> *The Lord bless thee, and keep thee:*
>
> *The Lord make his face shine upon thee, and be gracious unto thee:*
>
> *The Lord lift up his countenance upon thee, and give thee peace.*
>
> *And they shall put my name upon the children of Israel; and I will bless them.* NUMBERS 6:24-27

The Mezuzah: Jews today carry the Shma Israel as a credo in necklace charms or on the mezuzah nailed on the door posts of their buildings. The present day credo/name reads:

> *Hear, O Israel: The Lord our God is one Lord:*
>
> *And thou shalt love the Lord thy God with all thine heart, and with all thy soul, and with all thy might.*
>
> *And these words, which I command thee this day, shall be in thine heart:*

And thou shalt teach them diligently unto thy children, and shalt talk of them when thou sittest in thine house, and when thou walkest by the way, and when thou liest down, and when thou risest up.

And thou shalt bind them for a sign upon thine hand, and they shall be as frontlets between thine eyes.

And thou shalt write them upon the posts of thy house, and on thy gates.   DEUTERONOMY 6:4-9

Anthropomorphic God and Metal Plates: It may be concluded that the older credo, or name of God on the metal plates, implies a more anthropomorphic concept of God (face, countenance). The present credo coincides more with the modern Judaic idea that God cannot be comprehended with human understanding. In any case, after finding numerous plates and tablets, it is evident that the Israelites were writers and record keepers. It is still a custom to write memorials on metal plates.

The Jerusalem Cave at Lehi

Artifacts from a cave some twenty-three miles south and west of Jerusalem in an area known as *Lhi* (Lahi or Lehi) are dated to six hundred years before Jesus' time. The oldest-known writing of the name Jerusalem and the spelling out of the name Jehovah appears in this cave.

Book of Mormon Similarities: Three sentences suggested that the writers were hiding from enemies seeking their lives, seeking forgiveness for wrong doings, and hoping for a salvation of Jerusalem. These could be considered similar to a descriptive Book of Mormon account which Latter-day Saints claim is a record of a group of Jews leaving Jerusalem about six hundred years before Jesus' time.

A Man Named Lehi: A family of the area was instructed to leave Jerusalem. Their father, Lehi, was considered one of the prophets of the day.

For it came to pass in the commencement of the first year of the reign of Zedekiah, king of Judah, (my father, Lehi, having dwelt at Jerusalem in all his days); and in that same year there came many prophets, prophesying unto the people that they must repent, or the great city Jerusalem must be destroyed.   1 NEPHI 1:4

Lehi's Sons Hid in a Cave: Four brothers returned to Jerusalem to retrieve their family and religious records. The record keeper sent his servants to kill them. Hiding in a cave, two brothers rebelled and then were called to repentance by a heavenly messenger. The brothers may have sought forgiveness.

And it came to pass that we fled into the wilderness, and the servants of Laban did not overtake us, and we hid ourselves in the cavity of a rock.

And it came to pass that Laman was angry with me...

Old traditions become a part of everyday life as Jewish men walk down a street in Mea Shearim, the Orthodox section of Jerusalem. Many of the ancient Jewish traditions and customs have familiarity and special meaning for Latter-day Saints.

This round-roofed museum houses the scrolls found near the Dead Sea. The scrolls are kept at an even temperature and humidity 24 hours a day, under subdued special lighting, to preserve them for as long as possible.

> *And it came to pass as they smote us with a rod, behold, an angel of the Lord came and stood before them, and he spake unto them, saying: Why do ye smite your younger brother with a rod? Know ye not that the Lord hath chosen him to be a ruler over you, and this because of your iniquities? Behold ye shall go up to Jerusalem again, and the Lord will deliver Laban into your hands.*
> *1 NEPHI 3:27-29*

Jerusalem in Latter-days: The youngest of these brothers later becomes a prophet and speaks of Jerusalem in latter-days:

> *And now this I speak because of the spirit which is in me. And notwithstanding they have been carried away they shall return again, and possess the land of Jerusalem; wherefore, they shall be restored again to the land of their inheritance.   2 NEPHI 25:11*

Interestingly, that group was said to have been led by a man named Lehi.

Israelites to Leave and Return: Other archaeological discoveries also point to a history of Jews leaving or being led out of the land of Israel with promises that they would return. Similarly, there are biblical suggestions that Israelites would leave and return to the Holy Land.

> *Therefore, behold, the days come, saith the Lord, that it shall no more be said, The Lord liveth, that brought up the children of Israel out of the land of Egypt;*
>
> *But, The Lord liveth, that brought up the children of Israel from the land of the north, and from all the lands whither he had driven them: and I will bring them again into their land that I gave unto their fathers.   JEREMIAH 16:14-15*

Pontius Pilatus Stone

In the Israel Museum, remains of the first century include a stone tablet marking the residence of Pontius Pilatus, Prefect of Judea, at that time.

> *Now in the fifteenth year of the reign of Tiberius Caesar, Pontius Pilate being governor of Judaea...   LUKE 3:1*

Archaeological Evidence of Pontius Pilate: It is the only known archaeological evidence of Pontius Pilate of twenty centuries ago. The stone tablet was found in Caesarea, which was then the capital of the Roman province of Judea. The excavator was a colleague of mine and another fellow Israeli licensed guide. His business card reads, "Micha Ashkenazi...the man who found Pontius Pilate." The tablet had been toppled and later used by crusaders as a step in a staircase. Its writing, twenty centuries old, is still clearly visible.

The Dead Sea Scrolls and the Essenes

As mentioned in Chapter 9 about the Dead Sea, the most outstanding writing dating back twenty centuries is displayed in the Shrine of the Book. The discovery of the Dead Sea Scrolls by Bedouin shepherd boys led to the uncovering of the history of Jews who left Jerusalem about three hundred years before Jesus.

The Sons of Light: These religious Jews, known as Essenes, settled at the shore of the Salt Lake, now known as the Dead Sea. They called themselves "Sons (or children) of Light" and vaunted themselves in knowing the "signs of the times." Jesus may have referred to them when he said,

> ...*the children of this world are in their generation wiser than the children of light.   LUKE 16:8*

These "Sons of Light" removed themselves from society so they could worship privately. Their doctrine was to completely shun their enemies. Jesus may have referred to their isolationism when he said,

> *Ye have heard that it hath been said, Thou shalt love thy neighbour, and hate thine enemy.*
>
> *But I say unto you, Love your enemies, bless them that curse you, do good to them that hate you, and pray for them which despitefully use you, and persecute you;   MATTHEW 5:43-44*

Judaism, on the other hand, had specific instructions about giving enemies human consideration, probably to give them a possibility of change.

> *If thou meet thine enemy's ox or his ass going astray, thou shalt surely bring it back to him again.   EXODUS 23:4*
>
> *For if a man find his enemy, will he let him go well away? wherefore the Lord reward thee good for that thou hast done unto me this day.   1 SAMUEL 24:19*
>
> *Rejoice not when thine enemy falleth, and let not thine heart be glad when he stumbleth: PROVERBS 24:17*
>
> *If thine enemy be hungry, give him bread to eat; and if he be thirsty, give him water to drink: PROVERBS 25:21*

Essenes' Doctrine and Covenants: The leather scrolls in the Shrine of the Book at the Israel Museum are displayed in sealed cases where the humidity, temperature, and light are controlled. The writings on the scrolls show the expert penmanship of the Essenes.

Manual of Discipline: The best preserved of these Qumran scrolls is called *The Manual of Discipline*, a sort of "doctrine and covenants" of these religious people. It describes their organization that included a priestly system with two castes: - One

The Dead Sea Scrolls contain parts of
almost every book in the Old Testament,
including the entire book of Isaiah.
They also contain the interpretations,
doctrines, and covenants of what is
believed to be written by the Essenes.

of a higher authority that connected with an order of the Melech Zedek (righteous king) and another of lesser authority that connected with the Levitical, or order of Aaron. They were bound by a strict order of unity. An Essene's membership in a kibbutz-like united order came into effect only after a two-year trial period. The Essenes kept copies of the scriptures, interpretations of the scriptures, and their own scrolls of doctrines and covenants.

Teacher of Righteousness and Council of Twelve: The scroll of their principles and vows, *The Manual of Discipline*, describes their organization which included the office of a *Teacher of Righteousness* who had two assistants, a Council of Twelve overseers, as well as a system of higher and lesser authorities. Some people suggest that this governing system was copied by Jesus, and that he may have studied with this sect. It seems highly unlikely that this is the case. However, Jesus did use the same system of government that was given to Moses, a system that partially continued to exist in other Jewish traditions up to and at the time of Jesus.

> *And when it was day, he called unto him his disciples: and of them he chose twelve, whom also he named apostles;*   LUKE 6:13

> *After these things the Lord appointed other seventy also, and sent them two and two before his face into every city and place, whither he himself would come.*   LUKE 10:1

> *And he said unto Moses, Come up unto the Lord, thou, and Aaron, Nadab, and Abihu, and seventy of the elders of Israel; and worship ye afar off.*   EXODUS 24:1

Presidency of Three: The Qumran community did not follow the Mosaic governmental pattern completely. Jesus did. For example, Moses had a governing leadership of three persons, Moses and his two assistants, Aaron and Hur.

> *And he said unto the elders, Tarry ye here for us, until we come again unto you: and, behold, Aaron and Hur are with you: if any man have matters to do, let him come unto them.*   EXODUS 24:14

Moses had a governing body of twelve elders, one from each tribe.

> *These are those that were numbered... and the princes of Israel, being twelve men: each one was for the house of his fathers.*
> NUMBERS 1:44

This order was continued after Moses as well.

> *Now therefore take you twelve men out of the tribes of Israel, out of every tribe a man.*   JOSHUA 3:12

Considering Jesus as an Essene is speculation. To consider his organization as following an ancient biblical pattern is based on substantial information.

Back to Judaic Basics: Although their Judaic interpretations varied from Judaism and from the early doctrine of believers in Jesus, it is apparent the Essenes loved the scriptures and were making an attempt to get back to the basic fundamentals of

Moses' time. They may have even hoped God would send them a prophet. They created new psalms and wrote commentaries on the scriptures. The entire book of Isaiah is shown in photocopy form in a scroll-handle display. (Ancient scrolls were rolled on sticks.) References to writing on sticks or wood are also in the Bible.

Comparisons of Essene Judaism and Christianity: Meaningful comparisons of Judaism and Christianity today can be found in the similarity (or dissimilarity) of various doctrines and concepts. The Essenes referred to God in anthropomorphic (manlike) terms. The Messiah they anticipated was apparently known by previous prophets. In that sense, they inferred a premortal existence. Their teachings included a concept of a "united order" community where one would be a full member after a considerable testing time. Followers of Jesus committed immediately to such a similar order. The concept of "love your neighbor—hate your enemy" may have come from the Essenes' being so separate and so set apart. They would not even eat food that others had prepared or read scriptures that had not been copied by their own scribes. Jesus taught the opposite doctrine, to love your enemies; he even ate food with publicans and sinners.

Temple Scroll: The latest full document to come to light is the Temple Scroll. These "Sons of Light", as they called themselves, did not approve of the corruption in Jerusalem and its temple, so they redesigned and planned another one to be built in latter-days. There are prophecies of a latter-day temple in the scripture:

> *Moreover I will make a covenant of peace with them; it shall be an everlasting covenant with them: and I will place them, and multiply them, and will set my sanctuary in the midst of them for evermore.   EZEKIEL 37:26*

The Essenes in the Latter-days: The Essenes felt that they were actually in the latter-days. The terminology they used to refer to themselves is best translated as "saints" or "those set apart." (Although similar in usage today, there is no connection to the Latter-day Saints of modern times.) Just before Dr. Yigal Yadin passed away, this scholar of the Dead Sea Scrolls managed to finish and publish his work on the Temple Scroll that he acquired in 1967.

Links Between Jesus and the Essenes: Recent revelations of photographs of still-unpublished scroll fragments show that the manner of speaking and some doctrinal ideas of the Jews were also used at the time of Jesus. Some have suggested that there might be a link, but most scholars agree that the similarities do not prove or even suggest that Jesus or John the Baptist came from the Qumran community. As previously mentioned, what can be concluded is the possibility that the Essenes wanted to return to basic ancient Judaism with its previous organizational and doctrinal structure. Their Judaic similarities to Jesus are rather common sense within a common time frame.

SCRIPTURAL REFERENCES (KJV)

Section Five

*The four points, called the horns of the altar,
were important in the ceremony and played
a role in ancient sacrifices.*

Features of Jerusalem at the Time of Jesus

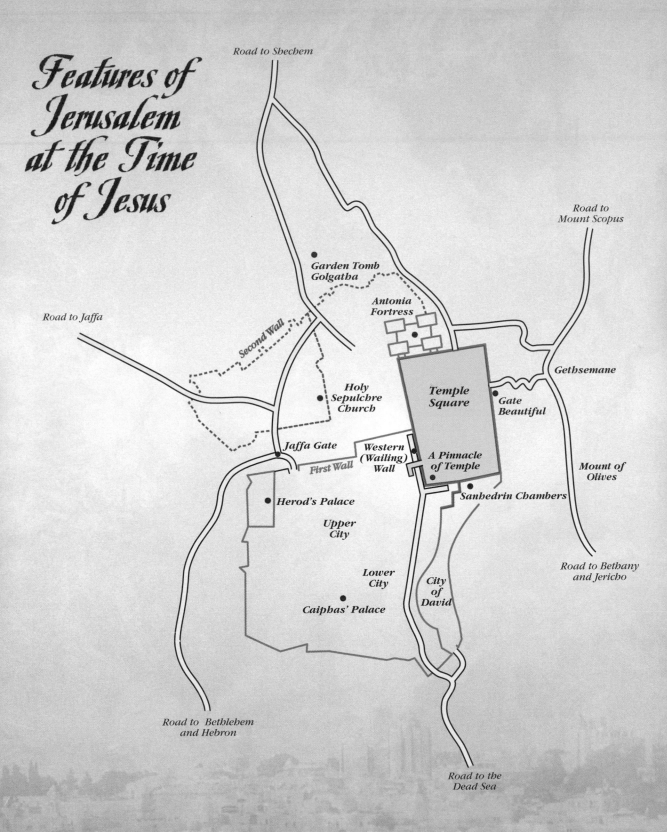

Road to Shechem

Road to Jaffa

Road to Mount Scopus

Garden Tomb Golgatha

Antonia Fortress

Second Wall

Gethsemane

Holy Sepulchre Church

Temple Square

Gate Beautiful

Jaffa Gate

First Wall

Western (Wailing) Wall

A Pinnacle of Temple

Mount of Olives

Herod's Palace

Sanhedrin Chambers

Upper City

Lower City

City of David

Caiphas' Palace

Road to Bethany and Jericho

Road to Bethlehem and Hebron

Road to the Dead Sea

SECTION SIX

- Overview -
Jerusalem in the
Footsteps of Jesus

Visualizing the hills of **BETHLEHEM** helps you clearly read and imagine the biblical accounts of Ruth, David, and the birth of Jesus. Examining the traditional birthplace, the **CHURCH OF THE NATIVITY**, will be a thought-provoking contrast to the quiet hillsides overlooking that important city. The rest of this section retraces the last week of Jesus' mortal ministry: **BETHANY** and **LAZARUS'S TOMB**; **THE MOUNT OF OLIVES** with a "triumphal entry" view of Jerusalem; an **UPPER ROOM**, where Jesus had a special Passover meal—the "Last Supper;" scenes of **THE GARDEN OF GETHSEMANE**, highlight the Atonement; **CAIAPHAS' PALACE**, site of the Jewish mock trial of Jesus; **ANTONIA FORTRESS**, where Pontius Pilate sat in judgment; the so-called **VIA DOLOROSA** (the way to the crucifixion); and then **THE GARDEN TOMB**, where Jesus was buried and rose again on the third day. These events, which follow the scriptural narrative, are spirit-filled experiences. This is the focus and highlight of **ISRAEL REVEALED**. The sights, sounds, and spirit of this land truly affect your life forever.

*A shepherdess and her child watch their flocks
exactly as was done anciently.*

Chapter 18

Bethlehem and Bethany

Religious Sites

 A Spiritual Guide to the Sites: There are more traditional sites with Jesus in and around Jerusalem than any other place in the world. While almost everyone else goes "site-seeing," let's really see Jerusalem from the "insight out." Using the scriptures, we will follow the events—carefully, simply; and what is most important, we will let the spirit guide us through the maze of tradition and competing sites. It is worth reminding ourselves that the most important task in learning is to recognize the truth. It is often quipped among tour guides that the more often a statement is repeated, the truer it becomes! However, for something as important as the Holy Land with its history and religion, I have suggested four simple considerations to be your guide. Let me repeat them: archaeology, written historical accounts, traditions, and feelings.

The account that follows can give you the true feelings of these sacred places. There is a sense of hallowedness and awe that time has not erased. It is because He is still here, in this Holy Land.

The heartfelt joy of the Holy Land comes from being at the locations and remembering the events that took place there.

"There is a sense of hallowedness and awe that time has not erased. It is because He is still here, in this Holy Land."

Bethlehem

Today many people travel to the Holy Land to look for Jesus in traditional spots. They expect a stable behind an inn. They come looking for scenes they learned from Christmas cards. Their traditional perceptions come from the West. Let's draw our attention to the East where it really happened. First, let's examine the traditional site. One foreign broadcast correspondent once commented about his Christmas visit in Israel. He said that Bethlehem should be spelled, B-E-D-L-A-M. The conflict, chaos, and confusion of Christmas Day were not what he had expected. After reviewing the traditional site, we can examine the not-so-well-known site where sheep and shepherds still roam on the hillsides of Bethlehem.

The Nativity Church: The traditionally accepted birthplace of Jesus is in a grotto located under the Church of Nativity. A grotto or cave is not improbable because stables were usually on the ground floor or underneath the inn rooms. Ancient inns were usually caravan stops. People were accustomed to "camping." There were a few private rooms—not at all like today's Holiday Inns. However, the word used by Luke to describe the "inn" is a "Katalyma," which means a guest chamber in someone's home. In that sense, even the relatives' or friends' guest chambers were already filled. The traditional site for Jesus' birthplace was established only 175 years after his birth. Three Christian churches, the Greek Orthodox, Armenian, and Catholic, hold separate services here and maintain a star decorating the place of birth. On a visit in 1972. President Harold B. Lee said while sitting in an adjacent room to the "birth grotto," "We are close to where the Savior was born."

Mixed Ownership of the Church: Ownership is tentative, at best. The three churches rotate their rights to use the grotto. Each church's priests, in turn, bring their own decorative accouterments, adornments, carpets, and curtains to be used during their particular mass or service. After that, they must remove all of their items, relinquishing temporary ownership to the next religious group. In the past, there have been considerable conflicts over these ownership rights. In 1989, a change was made among the Armenian priests. An Australian, Father Nursis, came to direct the Armenian Bethlehem facility. A good-natured man, he went directly to the Greek Orthodox and Catholic prelates and made friends. He has reconciled centuries of conflict. For example, the fight over ownership of a wall separating their two chapels has been resolved. Previously regular headlines around Christmas time would read, "Annual Christmas brawl breaks out at Bethlehem Church." Most of this seems to have been settled, mostly through the efforts of a friendly and faithful visiting priest. As of now, his temporary visit seems to be turning into a permanent stay in the Holy Land.

Manger Square and Mosques: During Christmas week, the square is full of bleachers for various visiting choral groups. Shops and the few trees nearby are festively decorated; the mosque is not. Opposite or close to every Christian church in this Holy Land is a Moslem mosque, and Bethlehem's Manger Square is no exception. Across the street, the municipal offices, souvenir shops, and new television antennas stretch up from aged housetops. The skyline picture is surely a contrast to what the village of Bethlehem must have looked like twenty centuries ago. Let's go back to that time.

Ruth and Naomi in Bethlehem: Around Bethlehem are numerous hills still grazed by sheep and goats. In the spring the small fields, supported by terraces, are planted with wheat or barley. It was these hills that the widows Naomi and Ruth returned to from Moab. Ruth gathered after the reapers; her good fortune was to work in the fields of Boaz, who was a relative of Naomi's late husband, Elimelech.

> *And Elimelech Naomi's husband died; and she was left, and her two sons.*

> *And they took them wives of the women of Moab; the name of the one was Orpah, and the name of the other Ruth....*

> *And Mahlon and Chilion died also both of them;...*

> *...she went forth out of the place where she was,...*

Discovered in the 1800's by General Gordon of Khartoum, the Garden Tomb is considered by many scholars to be the tomb of Jesus. This tomb fits all of the criteria mentioned in the New Testament and has a special spirit about it.

And she said, Behold, thy sister in law is gone back unto her people, and unto her gods: return thou after thy sister in law.

And Ruth said, Intreat me not to leave thee, or to return from following after thee: for whither thou goest, I will go; and where thou lodgest, I will lodge: thy people shall be my people, and thy God my God:

Where thou diest, will I die, and there will I be buried: the Lord do so to me, and more also, if ought but death part thee and me,

So Naomi returned, and Ruth the Moabitess...and they came to Bethlehem in the beginning of barley harvest.   RUTH 1:3-22

Ruth married Boaz and had a son named Obed, who had a son named Jesse, who tended flocks and crops in these same hills. It is still the Middle-East custom for the husband's family to care for the late husband's widowed wife. What Boaz did was culturally proper, and it certainly blossomed into a sweet love story.

And Naomi had a kinsman of her husband's, a mighty man of wealth...and his name was Boaz....

And Ruth...gleaned in the field after the reapers: and her hap was to light on a part of the field belonging unto Boaz, who was of the kindred of Elimelech....

Then said Boaz unto Ruth...abide here fast by my maidens...

Then she...said unto him, Why have I found grace in thine eyes,... seeing I am a stranger?

And Boaz answered...a full reward be given thee of the Lord God of Israel, under whose wings thou art come to trust.   RUTH 2:1-12

The Lineage of Kings: A genetic line began as he married Ruth, a foreign convert, and that set the stage for a line of kings.

So Boaz took Ruth, and she was his wife... and she bare a son....

And Naomi took the child, and laid it in her bosom, and became nurse unto it.

And the women her neighbours gave it a name, saying, There is a son born to Naomi; and they called his name Obed: He is the father of Jesse, the father of David.   RUTH 4:13, 16-17

King David: Jesse's youngest son was named David. In obscurity and in his child-hood he was ordained the King of Israel. Yet he continued to be a shepherd; surely he was a good shepherd. Born at Bethlehem, he was promised by God that his seed would bring the King of Kings, the Messiah—also to be known as the Good Shepherd.

I am the good shepherd: the good shepherd giveth his life for the sheep.   JOHN 10:11

A Latter-day David: David proved himself politically, militarily, and spiritually. In spite of his sinfulness later in his life, Israelis still sing about the old David, King of Israel, awaiting a new Davidic descendant. Virtually every Bar Mitzvah celebration is enhanced by singing to the Jewish lad being honored. He is treated as an expected David, one that should come in latter-days, out of obscurity, to reestablish a righteous kingdom. Christians feel that the Davidic prophecies began to be fulfilled when the Davidic kingdom was partially restored in the meridian of time with the coming of Jesus of Nazareth. They do expect the rest of the fulfillment to come later.

> *For unto us a child is born, unto us a son is given: and the government shall be upon his shoulder: and his name shall be called Wonderful, Counsellor, The mighty God, The everlasting Father, The Prince of Peace.*
>
> *Of the increase of his government and peace there shall be no end, upon the throne of David, and upon his kingdom, to order it, and to establish it with judgment and with justice from henceforth even for ever. The zeal of the Lord of hosts will perform this. ISAIAH 9:6-7*

In considering the words of Jeremiah, Ezekiel, and Hosea, the Jewish expectation of a latter-day David seems to include a person similar to the ancient David in addition to the Davidic Messiah, the King of Kings. For many he will also come out of obscurity.

> *But they shall serve the Lord their God, and David their king, whom I will raise up unto them. JEREMIAH 30:9*
>
> *And I the Lord will be their God, and my servant David a prince among them; I the Lord have spoken it. EZEKIEL 34:24*
>
> *Afterward shall the children of Israel return, and seek the Lord their God, and David their king; and shall fear the Lord and his goodness in the latter days. HOSEA 3:5*

If ancient events indicate patterns for the future, the latter-day David may be like the ancient David. He probably will prove himself politically, militarily, and spiritually. The people may then want to proclaim him a king. However, although honored in a high government position or as a prince or a noble person, he will introduce and bear witness of the King of Kings, who came in the meridian of time and will return in the latter-days to reign in the House of Israel forever.

The King of Kings

A simple story that comes from almost nowhere, out of obscurity, is the erstwhile introduction of the Davidic descendant, the King of Kings.

Born During Passover: Jesus was born in the Passover season, the spring of that year. According to the biblical calendar, Passover always occurs at the first full moon after the first day of spring. By the way, April 6, 1830 is the date The Church of Jesus Christ of Latter-day Saints was organized, and it was also the first full moon after the first day of spring.

From the hills surrounding Bethlehem, the city seems to look almost as it did two thousand years ago when the Savior was born in one of the caves outside the city. King David was also born in Bethlehem.

...being one thousand eight hundred and thirty years since the coming of our Lord and Savior Jesus Christ in the flesh....
DOCTRINE & COVENANTS 20:1

The Deliverer was born at the season celebrating both the deliverance of Israel from Egypt and an expectation of even a greater deliverance. The two deliverances are linked by a journey of time through two millennia.

The Journey to Bethlehem: The journey from Nazareth to Bethlehem had taken at least a week to ten days.

And it came to pass in those days, ...that Joseph also went ...unto the city of David, which is called Bethlehem...with Mary his espoused wife... LUKE 2:1-5

Bethlehem was their destination because they were of the house and lineage of David. They may have "camped" at a caravan inn or stayed with relatives for some time, before they inquired for a private room. The scripture reads,

And so it was, that, while <u>they were there</u>, the days were accomplished that she should be delivered.

And she brought forth her firstborn son, and wrapped him in swaddling clothes, and laid him in a manger; because there was no room for them in the inn. LUKE 2:6-7

Angels and Shepherds: Nearby, shepherds watched over their flocks, and angels announced good tidings.

For unto you is born this day in the city of David a Savior, which is Christ the Lord.

... Ye shall find the babe wrapped in swaddling clothes, lying in a manger. LUKE 2:11-12

Twenty centuries later, we feel that we may know some of those angels. Were we there? Was Naomi also happily singing? In her life she was bitter, having lost her husband and sons. But she brought a convert daughter-in-law to Bethlehem to become the great-great-grandmother of King David, whose royal line brings our Messiah. Our Savior came from a convert's family!

Modern Shepherds: Although most of the six million inhabitants of this little land of Israel do not know anything about him, I am grateful that I do. Some of my neighbors are shepherds, possibly descendants of ancient shepherds. My family and I have shared their happiness when their babies were born, as naturally as the baby lambs are born. We have mourned with them as their children die.

The Story of Jamil: One of those children was my little Arab friend Jamil with blonde hair and big brown eyes. For years, this silent child, dwarfed and barrel-chested by illness, stood by me every week as I told and read the story of Jesus' birth to tourists sitting with me on the hillsides with sheep and shepherds. Jamil even managed to smile a time or two. He did not understand the words, he could not hear nor could he speak, but he soaked in the spirit and love of our simple songs and unspoken love. Week after week, month after month, year after year, he came running out of his mother's tent to be with us.

One day there was no Jamil—and his mother would not come out of the tent. His cousin from a nearby tent explained, "Jamil died."

The next few weeks were not the same, although other children came to watch and listen to us. Life eventually seemed to return to normal, but his mother never seemed to lose the grief of Jamil's death. Months later she finally asked me, "Picture . . . Jamil?" I realized she missed him so. It took several months to locate someone who had taken a picture of Jamil. We had it enlarged and framed. Then one of our tourist guests, a modern Ruth, presented the photo to the shepherd mother.

Our Arab speaking driver explained to the shepherdess that Ruth had also lost her son just months before. Ruth offered the framed photo that contained an inscription, "Jamil is waiting for you and wants you to be happy." Our shepherdess, typically showing no emotion, took the picture. Then as the two women sank to the base of an olive tree, they softly wept. The shepherd mother slowly rocked back and forth, holding Jamil close to her. I saw that this began the end of her grief. I sensed that she believed the promise that was made.

We made the promise because we know that another child from Bethlehem made it possible for families to be reunited. We shared the thought that in the meantime, departed ones are still near at hand. For almost thirty years tourists and I have shared feelings and sung songs to these humble shepherds—songs that angels announced two thousand years ago. We cannot sing, "Far, far away on Judea's plains shepherds of old heard the joyous strains." The words come out as, "Near, near at hand on Judea's hills, shepherds of old heard the joyous trills!"

Today's shepherds may not yet understand our words, but one day they will, and they will understand the gift of the One born in a stable and laid in manger.

Bethany

The House of the Poor: About five miles north of Bethlehem and less than two miles east of Jerusalem is another ancient village called Bethany. The word *Bethani* means "house of the poor." There are still honorably poor people living here. Their faith is exemplary. For almost thirty years I have visited the poor crusader-built room of the widow of Abu Issa Mukahal, a Moslem married to a Christian Arab woman, Shifa. She has demonstrated her simple faith by raising eight children in that one room. Over the years, the children have added one more room and a kitchen hut. At last count, twenty-eight grandchildren assemble there almost daily or weekly. There is one full-time job and some scattered temporary jobs to support them all. Shifa often begins preparing food by reaming out carrots and small zucchini squashes to stuff them with rice and crumbs of ground meat—which she does not have. Her faith is that before the evening, a litle money will somehow trickle in, and she will be able to purchase the last ingredients. Some tourists do sense that Bethany is still home to the honorable poor and they give to the poor as a result.

Bethany was the home of Lazarus who was raised from death by the Savior. This little village was a favorite place for Jesus to stay. It is a short distance from here to the Mount of Olives and Jerusalem.

This rock-hewn tomb dates from the time of Jesus and is the traditional tomb of Lazarus. It has an entrance and steps made by Christians several hundred years ago.

Home of Lazarus: More commonly it is called *Al-Azaria*. This is derived from the two-thousand-year-old name of an inhabitant of Bethany who was called Eliezer. In modern English, his name became known as Lazarus. Traditional churches mark the events involving Mary, Martha, and Lazarus. These friends of Jesus anxiously awaited his swift return to their home. They had sent a message to him across the Jordan River that Lazarus was ill. (The message may have taken a journey at least one or two days to reach him, and Jesus would have needed at least another one or two days journey to return if he left immediately.) However,

> *When he had heard therefore that he was sick, he abode two days still in the same place where he was...*

> *Then when Jesus came, he found that he [Lazarus] had lain in the grave four days already.   JOHN 11:6-17*

The Tomb of Lazarus: The entrance and steps to Lazarus's tomb were made by Christians just hundreds of years ago. However, they do lead down through the crest of a hill to the remains of a first-century Jewish tomb. Typically, such tombs had two chambers. One chamber was for the mourners who would return for seven days, praying and weeping. (This mourning is called *Shiva* in Hebrew.) Another chamber was the burial room, wherein the bodies were placed within a day of passing away.

Raised from the Dead: After three days it was customary to close the burial room but to continue mourning for the rest of the seven-day period. Jesus asked,

> *...Where have ye laid him? They said unto him, Lord come and see.*

> *[Then] Jesus said, Take ye away the stone....*

> *[Jesus]...cried with a loud voice, Lazarus, come forth.*
> *JOHN 11:34-43*

Lazarus' family was amazed! They knew that within a day of his death, the body had been washed, completely immersed, and anointed with fragrant spiced oils. They probably assisted in dressing the body, fastening his hands and feet, and reverently wrapping the talith over his head and around his body. As they laid him in the burial chamber, they knew that he was dead, and now, before their very eyes, he was alive again. His "shuffling" out of the burial chamber must have astonished the mourners so much that Jesus had to reassure them:

> *...Loose him, and let him go.   JOHN 11:44*

Lazarus was one of several people Jesus raised from the dead. They would all eventually die again. Jesus himself would become the first to resurrect from the dead, never to die again. The raising of Lazarus aroused great interest among the people. The miracle was reported to the High Priests who immediately felt threatened. In their minds, Jesus' popularity imperiled their social and political standing. A council convened, and Caiaphas, the High Priest that year, suggested that Jesus should die.

Caiaphas further justified his wicked proposal by exclaiming that Jesus' popularity was spreading to other Jews in other lands. Again, that would imperil Caiaphas' influence throughout the Jewish world.

Martha and Mary: What happened after Lazarus was raised is only recorded as a short journey to a city called Ephraim, where Jesus and the disciples tarried for awhile. Some time later, six days before the Passover, Jesus returned to Bethany to have dinner with Lazarus, Martha, and Mary. It was at this occasion that Mary anointed the feet of Jesus.

Judas Iscariot Objects: Judas Iscariot objected to such a waste of expensive ointment. After all, there were so many poor people. Jesus responded,

> *...Let her alone: against the day of my burying hath she kept this.*

> *For the poor always ye have with you; but me ye have not always.*
> *JOHN 12:7-8*

The near future would show that this anointing was done in preparation of his own burial. Incidentally, the name *Iscariot* may mean the "man of Kirya." (*Ish* means "man", and *Kirya*—nowadays—refers to "a city"). Interestingly, this disciple was the only one of the twelve that did not come from the Galilee. He was the "man of the city," in colloquialism *a city slicker.*

Schemes to Execute Lazarus and Jesus: Many people came out of their cities to see both Jesus and Lazarus. Lazarus had become a tourist attraction. That is when the High Priests began scheming to have Lazarus executed as well. His popularity was drawing people toward Jesus. The High Priest justified his wish that Jesus should be killed by suggesting,

> *...this man doeth many miracles.*

> *If we let him thus alone, all men will believe on him: and the Romans shall come and take away both our place and nation.*

> *...it is expedient for us, that one man should die...that the whole nation perish not.*

> *...they took counsel together for to put him to death.*
> *JOHN 11:47-53*

The death of Jesus was on the minds of the priests while they were preparing for a festival of deliverance. They even began scheming about how Lazarus could be eliminated, for surely his account of "life after life" drew too much attention. Events were coming together that would change the world. It was less than a week before Passover.

> *Then Jesus six days before the passover came to Bethany, where Lazarus was which had been dead, whom he raised from the dead....*

> *Much people of the Jews therefore knew that he was there: and they came not for Jesus' sake only, but that they might see Lazarus also, whom he had raised from the dead.*

> *But the chief priests consulted that they might put Lazarus also to death;*

> *Because that by reason of him many of the Jews went away, and believed on Jesus. JOHN 12:1, 9-11*

Chapter 19

The Preparation

Triumphal Entry

 Five days before the Passover, Jesus sent his disciples to the neighboring village of Bethphage to find a donkey. They returned with two animals, a donkey and its colt. Jesus chose to ride the colt. The sight of a large man riding a small donkey is startling enough. However, the gesture must have called up historical images of honored kings riding into Jerusalem on lowly donkeys that had never been ridden before. To some, this may have implied that Jesus was their King. The people, hearing that Jesus was coming to Jerusalem, then took branches of palm trees, a well-known symbol of Jewish independence, and cried as,

> *...they heard that Jesus was coming . . . Hosanna: Blessed is the King of Israel that cometh in the name of the Lord.* JOHN 12:12-13

Palm Sunday and the Passover: His triumphal entry on a donkey's colt down the Mount of Olives and into the Gate Beautiful raised the spirits of the Jews. They wanted a Messiah, and they praised this extraordinary man of miracles. Simultaneously, priests were angered and decided to set in motion a plan to have Jesus executed. The triumphal entry has been called Palm Sunday; and again, it was five days before the Passover that year. Jewish biblical days begin at evening—first there is nighttime and then there is the daylight portion. This is probably based on the creation sequence; at first it was a dark void and then it was day. God made the day after it was night.

> *And God called the light Day, and the darkness he called Night. And the evening and the morning were the first day.* GENESIS 1:5

This brief explanation can help one visualize the sequence of events leading up to the Passover day that year, a High Day, that as all other days ran evening to evening.

The Passover

Passover Preparations: Since the Passover was coming soon, preparations for cleaning, and removal of all leaven, yeast, or items that might sprout or rise were under way. A tradition still followed in modern Israel is that the leaven must be "sold." The chief rabbi arranges to sell the entire country's supply of grain, prepackaged breads,

"His clothing surely must have been stained red. Symbolizing the ancient biblical practice of sacrificing a red-haired, unblemished firstborn calf on this mount."

and leavened products to a non-Jew before the Passover begins. Therefore, whatever leaven is still around does not really belong to the Jews. The deal usually includes that this Gentile will collect all the leaven (or what might rise) when his payment is complete. However, after only a token down payment, the non-Jew, a nonbeliever, never really gets around to making the final payment. So, by default, ownership is "returned" to the Jews; it just happens, meanwhile, that the Passover is completed anyway. With the Passover preparation in mind, the disciples asked,

> *...Where wilt thou that we prepare for thee to eat the passover?*
> *MATTHEW 26:17*

The Upper Room: He instructed them to find a man carrying a water pitcher; this is something women usually would do. They found the man who led them to an upper room. Most people just assume that the upper room was upstairs. Jerusalem had two city parts known as the upper city and the lower city. It is possible that the term upper room really refers to a room in the upper part of the city where many prominent priests lived. The disciples said,

> *...The Master saith, My time is at hand; I will keep the passover at*
> *thy house with my disciples.   MATTHEW 26:18*

From what follows in the scriptural narrative, the preparations may have been ready except for the sacrificial lamb. There are no sacrifices made or eaten during the preparation time until the ninth hour of the day (about three hours before Passover begins).

Passover Traditions: To better understand Jesus' "Last Supper," consideration of other highlights of the Passover will be helpful. In the past, the *Seder* table was set up in a U-shape with the participants sitting on the outside. So, looking inward, the master of the house, usually the oldest male, would sit second from the right end. This kept available an empty spot to his right. It is still the custom that the oldest will usually select a boy, probably the youngest, to sit at his right hand and assist him in the order (Seder) of the meal and ritual customs. One duty of the boy is to sing a song, "What makes this night different from any other night?" Later, we will consider three differences of Jesus' Passover from any other Passover.

Elijah at the Passover: Continuing with the seating arrangement, the last seat on the other end remains empty. It is available for Elijah. His place is opposite of the oldest and the youngest. Incidentally, the imagery and symbolism are outstanding. The Passover turns the hearts of the youngest to the traditions and deliverance of the past. Elijah's mission is to announce the coming of the "Deliverer."

> *Behold, I will send you Elijah the prophet before the coming of the*
> *great and dreadful day of the Lord:*
>
> *And he shall turn the heart of the fathers to the children, and the*
> *heart of the children to their fathers,...   MALACHI 4:5-6*

At the Master's Right Hand: An event occurring before the Passover two thousand years ago was a discussion of who would sit at the right hand of Jesus, the Master.

Olive tree and red lilies of the field near the Garden of Gethsemane

Then came to him the mother of Zebedee's children with her sons, worshipping him, and desiring a certain thing of him.

...Grant that these my two sons may sit, the one on thy right hand, and the other on the left,...

... Jesus answered... to sit on my right hand, and on my left, is not mine to give, but it shall be given to them for whom it is prepared of my Father.   MATTHEW 20:20-23

Jesus further taught,

And whosoever will be chief among you, let him be your servant: MATTHEW 20:27

Thus, the ancient Passover seating arrangement became quite significant. Could the question have been a practical one for that Passover occasion? Which of the youngest would sit by the Master?

Foods for the Passover: Considering the Jewish calendar and the scriptural narrative, Jesus then led a Passover meal with his disciples in the upper room. It still was only the beginning of the preparation evening/day. The Passover really began on the following evening. Modern-day preparations include bitter herbs that are symbolic of bondage. There is a mixture of chopped fruit, nuts, cinnamon, and honey that represent deliverance. Parsley or watercress is used as a token of gratitude for the earth's abundant goodness.   Salted water or vinegar is set out for cleansing use. There are also preparations of a lamb's shank bone, a reminder of past sacrifices.   There is an egg, also reminiscent of a sacrifice and new beginning.

Symbolism of Foods: At Passover, these and other certain foods are eaten, symbolizing the deliverance from Egypt. Wine is prepared, and it will be used four times. A prominent rabbi in Israel recently suggested that even the wine should be "unleavened" or unfermented. This could be considered "new wine." The ancient metaphor of new wine was also used to anticipate the Deliverer. Ancient prophets said,

Awake, ye drunkards, and weep; and howl, all ye drinkers of wine, because of the new wine...   JOEL 1:5

And it shall come to pass in that day, that the mountains shall drop down new wine...   JOEL 3:18

No man also having drunk old wine straightway desireth new: for he saith, The old is better.   LUKE 5:39

Wine and Bread Symbolism: Analyzing the symbolism, one can suggest that when wine is poured before the bread is broken, it is done to remember the first Passover deliverance. However, what is more important, it is done to look forward to a greater deliverance in the future. In the Seder, there are three times when the wine is blessed and sipped. Following each wine sip, a piece of unleavened bread is used. Each piece is blessed, broken, and eaten.   There is a total of three pieces of bread, but they are used four times. Toward the beginning of the Seder, the middle of three pieces is first broken in two. Half has to be hidden away, usually in an upper part of the house. In

During Passover, the area around the Western Wall becomes crowded with Jewish pilgrims from all over the world. They come here to commemorate the ancient deliverance of the Jews from Egypt.

any case, it must be hidden "above" something—preferable to hiding it "underneath" something. It will be found later by children and it will be used with a fourth cup of wine. However, in many traditions, this fourth cup of wine is used after the fourth piece of bread, the *Afikomen*, is found.

Door Left Open for Elijah: A complete meal is eaten with a door left open for Elijah, who, by Jewish tradition, would announce the coming Messiah. After the meal, children search for the hidden piece of bread that is often wrapped in a red cloth. When found, the children receive a gift. This piece of bread is then blessed, broken, and eaten. Some traditions use this last piece of bread, the Afikomen, to dip in the very sweet mixture of fruit and nuts, the *Charoseth*. As mentioned, it is after the Afikomen is found that the fourth cup of wine is poured and blessed. The master of the house then says, "Drink all of it." The prayer spoken then invokes a hope for a greater deliverance in the future.

Judas at the Last Supper: Let us return to the "Last Supper" of Jesus with his disciples. Sometime that evening, Judas excused himself and left. The other disciples may have thought he was going out to purchase the lamb for the Passover meal. Instead, he was leaving to "sell" the Lamb of God. Looking at the event in another way, one can see that his departure was to make a sale—for thirty pieces of silver he was selling the "Bread of Life" to the corrupt priests. Metaphorically we can see it as an act of selling the "Leaven, the Bread of Life," to unbelievers.

> *And offer a sacrifice of thanksgiving with leaven, and proclaim and publish the free offerings: for this liketh you, O ye children of Israel, saith the Lord GOD.   AMOS 4:5*

> *Purge out therefore the old leaven, that ye may be a new lump, as ye are unleavened. For even Christ our passover is sacrificed for us: 1 CORINTHIANS 5:7*

Jesus Preempts the Passover Meal: It seems that Jesus' supper preceded the normal time for the Passover meal that year by a day. That is the first item that was different this night than any other Passover night. The following evening really began the seven-day Passover period, and by that time Jesus was already crucified and in the tomb. This high, holy week always began on the first full moon after the first day of spring. Every year, that day becomes an extra Sabbath that week; it is called a High Day. That High Day may occur on any day of the week, including the regular Sabbath. However, what is most important is that the beginning and ending day of the Passover is always treated as a Sabbath day.

Bread and Wine Explained: The second item that makes the "Last Supper" different from any other night is the explanation of the bread taken before the wine. Jesus used this meal to teach his Apostles that he was the Deliverer. He probably showed that the Passover practice of partaking of wine followed by bread (three times) was very likely a symbolic anticipation of a future atonement. We can call this ordinance "old wine." It was henceforth changed to bread followed by wine—a symbolic remembrance of the deliverance he was to carry out within the next four days. We can call this ordinance "new wine." The Savior then,

The Last Supper was held in a so-called upper room in Jerusalem. This traditional room was built only 800 years ago, but it does remind us of the upper room mentioned in the scriptures.

> *...took bread, and gave thanks, and brake it, and gave unto them,*
> *saying, This is my body which is given for you: this do in remem-*
> *brance of me.   LUKE 22:19*

> *And he took the cup, and gave thanks, and gave it to them, saying,*
> *Drink ye all of it;   MATTHEW 26:27*

He also said,

> *For this is in remembrance of my blood of the new testament,*
> *which is shed for as many as shall believe on my name, for the*
> *remission of their sins.   MATTHEW 26:24 (JST)*

Messianic Symbol of Bread: The messianic symbolism can be further visualized in the three pieces of unleavened bread that could represent God, his Son, and the Holy Ghost. The three pieces are usually layered top, center, and bottom. In due course of the meal, the first part of the center piece is blessed (initially) and then broken. The hidden part of the center piece is found later (often wrapped in a red cloth) at the end of the meal by the children (a later generation), and then they receive a reward. That piece is then broken and then blessed, followed by wine. Another chiasmus can be recognized as first it is "wine and bread" then, after the "hidden" piece is found, it is "bread and wine." The Atonement is the center focus of "old wine" and "new wine" (both are names of the Lord). The tradition of placing the hidden piece above something may also connote the second coming of the Messiah. The first time, he came in lowly circumstances, and the second time he will come dressed in red and in great glory from above.   It is the later generation that finds him and "great shall be their reward."

The Traditional Upper Room: A traditional room built only eight hundred years ago reminds us of an upper room, as the scriptures say. As mentioned already, the word upper may refer to the upper part of the city rather than a room upstairs. The upper part of ancient Jerusalem was the area where the priests lived, and generally it was considered the upper-class section of the city. It was the section where many "temple Levites" lived. It was also close to the house of Annas, the former High Priest, and his son-in-law, Caiaphas.

Jesus as a Servant: The upper room Passover meal concluded with Jesus demonstrating his role as their servant.

> *After that he poureth water into a bason, and began to wash the*
> *disciples' feet, and to wipe them with the towel wherewith he was*
> *girded.   JOHN 13:5*

Peter objected, and Jesus responded,

> *...If I wash thee not, thou hast no part with me.*

> *Simon Peter saith unto him, Lord, not my feet only, but also my*
> *hands and my head.   JOHN 13:8-9*

Always teaching, the Savior continued,

> *If I then, your Lord and Master, have washed your feet; ye also*
> *ought to wash one another's feet.   JOHN 13:14*

This approximately two thousand year-old olive tree from the traditional Garden of Gethsemane reminds us of the Savior's agony. Studies indicate that the actual garden was located further up on the Mount of Olives.

A New Commandment: There was another instruction given during this evening that was different from instruction given any other time. This is the third item that made this night different than any other night.

> *A new commandment I give unto you, That ye love one another;*
> *as I have loved you,...   JOHN 13:34*

From Sinai where the children of Israel compromised themselves to the "lesser law of performance," the old concept was different,

> *Therefore all things whatsoever ye would that men should do to*
> *you, do ye even so to them: for this is the law and the prophets.*
> *MATTHEW 7:12*

Gethsemane

After their Passover meal, Jesus and eleven Apostles went to the Mount of Olives. The following prophetic conversation could have occurred on the way.

> *And when they had sung an hymn, they went out into the mount*
> *of Olives.*
>
> *Then saith Jesus unto them, All ye shall be offended because of me*
> *this night: for it is written, I will smite the shepherd, and the sheep*
> *of the flock shall be scattered abroad.*
>
> *But after I am risen again, I will go before you into Galilee.*
>
> *Peter answered and said unto him, Though all men shall be*
> *offended because of thee, yet will I never be offended.*
>
> *Jesus said unto him, Verily I say unto thee, That this night, before*
> *the cock crow, thou shalt deny me thrice.*
>
> *Peter said unto him, Though I should die with thee, yet will I not*
> *deny thee. Likewise also said all the disciples.*
>
> *Then cometh Jesus with them unto a place called Gethsemane, and*
> *saith unto the disciples, Sit ye here, while I go and pray yonder.*
> *MATTHEW 26:30-36*

Traditional Sites: Today there are several traditional churches in Gethsemane: Russian Orthodox, Greek Orthodox, and Catholic. The garden of the Catholic Church has had olive trees existing for the better part of twenty centuries. The garden mentioned in the scriptures was *Gethsemane*, a word that means a "winepress" or "olive press," usually found in a vineyard or orchard.

Agony at Gethsemane: The agony that Jesus went through became so difficult that he pleaded with the Father for relief, yet submissively said,

> *...O my Father, if this cup may not pass away from me, except I*
> *drink it, thy will be done. ...and prayed the third time, saying the*
> *same words.   MATTHEW 26:42, 44*

He perspired great drops of blood.

> *And being in an agony he prayed more earnestly: and his sweat*
> *was as it were great drops of blood falling down to the ground.*
> *LUKE 22:44*

Red Clothing: It seems that his clothing surely must have been stained red. His "red" (bleeding) may have been symbolized by the ancient biblical practice of sacrificing a red-haired, unblemished firstborn calf on this mount. The ashes of that red-haired calf were used in immersions of those needing a remission of sins.

> *This is the ordinance of the law which the Lord hath commanded...*
> *bring thee a red heifer without spot, wherein is no blemish,...*
>
> *And one shall burn the heifer in his sight;...*
>
> *And a man that is clean shall gather up the ashes of the heifer, and*
> *lay them up without the camp in a clean place, and it shall be kept*
> *for the congregation of the children of Israel for a water of*
> *separation: it is a purification for sin.   NUMBERS 19:2-9*

The Red Calf: In Jewish tradition, the place where the red calf was sacrificed was as high as one could get on the Mount of Olives to be above the temple. It was also in line with the Gate Beautiful and in a line that was northward of the temple altar. It is thus likely that Jesus' Gethsemane experience may have happened at the same location, further up the mount, rather than in the traditional places at the bottom of the mountain.

The Suffering of Jesus: The suffering of Jesus cannot be explained. He prayed again and again. Even he was astonished at the overwhelming suffering he had to bear.

> *...My soul is exceeding sorrowful, even unto death: tarry ye here,*
> *and watch with me.*
>
> *And he went a little further, and fell on his face, and prayed,*
> *saying, O my Father, if it be possible, let this cup pass from me:*
> *nevertheless not as I will, but as thou wilt....*
>
> *He went away again the second time, and prayed, saying, O my*
> *Father, if this cup may not pass away from me, except I drink it,*
> *thy will be done.*
>
> *...and went away again, and prayed the third time, saying the*
> *same words.   MATTHEW 26:38-44*

Red Symbols: An additional messianic symbol of that suffering is Isaiah's prophecy of the Messiah's arrival in red clothing on the Mount of Olives.

Lilies of Red

The season bursts forth in radiance,
    painting the landscape in shades of green.
    Flowers add their rythym in cadence,
        splashing color to brighten the scene.

        Most precious are the lilies of red.
            They spin not, they toil not, yet in their way,
            they teach of the color of Him who bled,
            on Gethsemane's most fateful day.

        His glory is to lighten our load.
        He heals us with joy and harmony .
    A landscape of love for young and old,
His radiance opened eternity.

Chorus:

Lilies of red, they testified
    of Him who bled and died,
        Lilies of red, witness they give
        He died so we could live.
        He lives, he's risen from the dead
praise God for Lilies of Red.

— Daniel Rona

Lilies of the field.

Who is this that cometh from Edom, with dyed garments from Bozrah? this that is glorious in his apparel, travelling in the greatness of his strength? I that speak in righteousness, mighty to save.

Wherefore art thou red in thine apparel, and thy garments like him that treadeth in the winefat?   ISAIAH 63:1-2

And it shall be said: Who is this that cometh down from God in heaven with dyed garments; yea, from the regions which are not known, clothed in his glorious apparel, traveling in the greatness of his strength?

And he shall say: I am he who spake in righteousness, mighty to save.

And the Lord shall be red in his apparel, and his garments like him that treadeth in the wine-vat.
DOCTRINE & COVENANTS 133:46-48

Another chiastic lesson seems obvious. Sacrifices of the red calves (whose ashes were used for purification of sins) were made on the Mount of Olives in ancient times. The expected arrival of the Messiah, in red, on the Mount of Olives will be in the latter days. The "red" (bleeding) experience of Jesus (who paid for everyone's sins) on the Mount of Olives was in the meridian of time. It is the central lesson of these events.

Chapter 20

Death and Resurrection

Caiaphas and the Trial of Jesus

A Mock Trial: Late that night, Jesus was betrayed, arrested, and taken to Caiaphas the High Priest, by his soldiers. The incarceration and interrogation were not part of an official trial. Both were illegal under the circumstances. That night was the first half of the Preparation Day, a holiday by itself; it was nighttime and there was no formal charge against Jesus. These and other items precluded any trial to be carried out legally.

> *And while he yet spake, lo, Judas, one of the twelve, came, and with him a great multitude with swords and staves, from the chief priests and elders of the people.*
>
> *Now he that betrayed him gave them a sign, saying, Whomsoever I shall kiss, that same is he: hold him fast.*
>
> *And forthwith he came to Jesus, and said, Hail, master; and kissed him.*
>
> *And Jesus said unto him, Friend, wherefore art thou come? Then came they, and laid hands on Jesus, and took him....*
>
> *In that same hour said Jesus to the multitudes, Are ye come out as against a thief with swords and staves for to take me? I sat daily with you teaching in the temple, and ye laid no hold on me.*
>
> *But all this was done, that the scriptures of the prophets might be fulfilled. Then all the disciples forsook him, and fled.*
>
> *And they that had laid hold on Jesus led him away to Caiaphas the high priest, where the scribes and the elders were assembled.*
>
> *But Peter followed him afar off unto the high priest's palace, and went in, and sat with the servants, to see the end.*
> *MATTHEW 26:47-58*

"For almost thirty years now, I have had the privilege of bringing people to an empty tomb."

Caiaphas, the High Priest: Caiaphas was the High Priest over three councils that made up the grand Sanhedrin assembly. However, Caiaphas apparently was only meeting with one of the councils and not the entire Sanhedrin (seventy men). The Sanhedrin would have to judge such a case, if it were a legal trial.

The House of Caiaphas: Caiaphas's house is now a church built over dungeon

*Ancient steps leading to Caiaphas' residence, and
one of the few sites revealed from beneath today's
ground level and the rubble of time. It is almost
certain that the Savior trod some of these steps on
His way to be tried by Caiaphas' council.*

rooms, two thousand years old, where prisoners were held. Holes in the rock walls were used to tie and spread out their hands and feet for scourging. This basement prison reminds us that Caiaphas and some powerful elders conspired to trap Jesus by his own words.

> *But Jesus held his peace...   MATTHEW 26:63*

Blasphemy: The priestly wordsmiths, who would not even say "God" or utter his name, had the practice of substituting words representing God's name. They would use phrases such as, "He that comes in the clouds of Heaven." They would refer to a messiah as "He that sits on the right hand of Power," or "Blessed is His name." In anger, the High Priest challenged him.

> *...I adjure thee by the living God, that thou tell us whether thou be the Christ, the Son of God.   MATTHEW 26:63*

Jesus simply replied,

> *...Thou hast said: nevertheless I say unto you, hereafter shall ye see [this] Son of man sitting on the right hand of power, and coming in the clouds of heaven.   MATTHEW 26:64*

The High Priest, perhaps stung by the realization that he himself had invoked God's name, cried out,

> *...He hath spoken blasphemy...*

> *What think ye? They answered and said, He is guilty of death. MATTHEW 26:65-66*

Peter Denies the Savior: The cock had just crowed. In fulfillment of Jesus' prophecy, Peter had just denied the Savior the third time. One can imagine as Peter turned and looked into Jesus' face, he ran out into the break of dawn, weeping bitterly.

> *Then began he to curse and to swear, saying, I know not the man. And immediately the cock crew.*

> *And Peter remembered the word of Jesus, which said unto him, Before the cock crow, thou shalt deny me thrice. And he went out, and wept bitterly.   MATTHEW 26:74-75*

Execution for Temple Violations: Under the Roman political system, the Jewish priests were not to carry out executions except for temple violations. (Their executions would have been by stoning, throwing the victim over a high cliff and then covering him with stones they threw down.) The priests bound him and led him away to Pontius Pilate, the governor.

Pontius Pilate

The Judgment Hall: Today, the site is maintained by a Catholic Order, *The Sisters of Zion*. The archaeological ruins recently discovered may have been well-preserved by the traditions dating from Byzantine times. Floor stones and cisterns reveal ancient Roman markings and usage as a fortress.

A Wife's Dream: At the Antonia Fortress, Pontius Pilate at first did not want to be troubled with the case. He may have been bothered by his wife's dream to have nothing to do with Jesus. However, he soon realized a potential political gain. He had Jesus brought forth, beaten, intimidated, and crowned with thorns. He repeatedly taunted the priests with Jesus' release. He said,

> *...I find in him no fault at all.   JOHN 18:38*

Crucify Him: Maddened by Pilate's reluctance to favor them with an execution, they cried out,

> *...Away with him, crucify him...   JOHN 19:15*

Political Gain: Pilate, probably goading them on and hoping to accomplish something for himself, said,

> *...Shall I crucify your King? The chief priests answered, We have no king but Caesar.   JOHN 19:15*

Ah, the political gain was achieved (the priests, after all, did publicly acclaim Caesar to be their king).

> *Then delivered he him...to be crucified...   JOHN 19:16*

This may have been the achievement that endeared Pilate to Herod—after all, he got the Jewish priests to acclaim Caesar.

> *And the same day Pilate and Herod were made friends together: for before they were at enmity between themselves.   LUKE 23:12*

The Crucifixion

The Place of a Skull: Jesus, bearing his cross (probably just the cross beam, as the upright post was most likely already at the crucifixion place),

> *...went forth into a place called the place of a skull, which is called in the Hebrew Golgotha: JOHN 19:17*

Simon from Cyrene: On the way, a man named Simon from Cyrene was made to carry the cross beam to the place of execution. (One can imagine that Jesus may have stumbled, although it is not mentioned.) The name Simon is Jewish; the place, Cyrene, is in Africa. The man could have been a black-skinned man, one of the hundreds of thousands of Jews of various ethnicities gathering in Jerusalem for Passover. He carried the wood for the sacrifice of the Paschal (Passover) Lamb of God.

*This gruesome-looking hill seems to
resemble the eye-sockets of death.
It graphically reminds us of the suffering
of Christ. It is known as a place of
stoning and execution of ancient times.
This site may be the actual Golgotha
of the crucifixion.*

Outside the City Wall: A site outside the city wall looks like the described place. It was the Roman practice to crucify along the roadways. In this ancient, abandoned quarry, known by Jews as a place of execution, a roadway still passes through.

Daylight had progressed about six hours. It was close to noon, but,

> *...there was darkness over the whole land until the ninth hour.*
> *MARK 15:33*

A Slow Death: Crucifixion was a slow, strangling death. Breathing required very painful movements, and speaking was extremely difficult. Yet, during his agonizing physical, mental, and spiritual anguish, he spoke several times. Mostly it was with concern for others.

Jesus Speaks from the Cross: The Bible records seven things that Jesus said while on the cross.

To those who nailed him:

> *Then said Jesus, Father, forgive them; for they know not what they do. And they parted his raiment, and cast lots.   LUKE 23:34*

To those crucified with him:

> *And one of the malefactors which were hanged railed on him, saying, If thou be Christ, save thyself and us.*
>
> *But the other answering rebuked him, saying, Dost thou not fear God, seeing thou art in the same condemnation?*
>
> *And we indeed justly; for we receive the due reward of our deeds: but this man hath done nothing amiss.*
>
> *And he said unto Jesus, Lord, remember me when thou comest into thy kingdom.*
>
> *And Jesus said unto him, Verily I say unto thee, Today shalt thou be with me in paradise [world of spirits].   LUKE 23:39-43*

To His Mother:

> *When Jesus therefore saw his mother, and the disciple standing by, whom he loved, he saith unto his mother, Woman, behold thy son! JOHN 19:26*

To John the Beloved:

> *Then saith he to the disciple, Behold thy mother! And from that hour that disciple took her unto his own home.   JOHN 19:27*

To the Guards:

> *After this, Jesus knowing that all things were now accomplished, that the scripture might be fulfilled, saith, I thirst.   JOHN 19:28*

To His Father:

> *And about the ninth hour Jesus cried with a loud voice, saying, Eli, Eli, lama sabachthani? that is to say, My God, my God, why hast thou forsaken me? MATTHEW 27:46*

> *And when Jesus had cried with a loud voice, he said, Father, into thy hands I commend my spirit: and having said thus, he gave up the ghost. LUKE 23:46*

To the World:

> *When Jesus therefore had received the vinegar, he said, It is finished: and he bowed his head, and gave up the ghost. JOHN 19:30*

His Legs Not Broken: The Jewish priests did not want the crucified bodies hanging on the crosses on the Sabbath days (for that evening was the beginning of an extra Sabbath day, a High Day). So, they besought Pilate that the prisoners' legs might be broken. This would hasten their deaths because they could not push upward, pressing against the nails in their feet to gasp for breath. Once dead, their bodies might be taken away. However, when the soldiers saw that Jesus was already dead,

> *...they brake not his legs: JOHN 19:33*

This also fulfilled a messianic prophecy which says:

> *He keepeth all his bones: not one of them is broken. PSALM 34:20*

A Tomb in a Garden

Disciples of Jesus Help with the Burial: After this, Joseph of Arimathaea, a member of the Sanhedrin, and

> *...a disciple of Jesus... besought Pilate that he might take away the body of Jesus: and Pilate gave him leave... JOHN 19:38*

With the help of Nicodemus,

> *...took they the body of Jesus, and wound it in linen clothes with the spices,...*

> *Now in the place where he was crucified there was a garden; and in the garden a new sepulchre, wherein was never man yet laid.*

> *There laid they Jesus therefore because of the Jews' preparation day; for the sepulchre was nigh at hand. JOHN 19:40-42*

Two Sabbaths in a Row: The scurrilous events of that day preceded the Passover which was due to begin any moment. The Passover (a special Sabbath or High Day) that week probably preceded the regular Saturday Sabbath.

> *The Jews [Priests] therefore, because it was the preparation, that the bodies should not remain upon the cross on the sabbath day, (for that sabbath day was an high day,)... JOHN 19:31*

A Sign to the Pharisees: It is probable that there were two Sabbaths in a row that year (the Passover Sabbath and the regular seventh day of the week Sabbath). In that sense, Jesus was crucified on what we call a Thursday. (This fits in the time reckoning of Palm Sunday being five days before the Passover.) Then in fulfillment of prophecy, he was in the tomb three nights; and on the third day he arose—

> *...and be raised again the third day.*
> *MATTHEW 16:21 (see also MATTHEW 17:23; MARK 9:31)*

This is also the only "sign" Jesus gave the Pharisees.

> *Then certain of the scribes and of the Pharisees answered, saying, Master, we would see a sign from thee.*
>
> *But he answered and said unto them, An evil and adulterous generation seeketh after a sign; and there shall no sign be given to it, but the sign of the prophet Jonas:*
>
> *For as Jonas was three days and three nights in the whale's belly; so shall the Son of man be three days and three nights in the heart of the earth.   MATTHEW 12:38-40*

In speaking to the Pharisees, he specifically connected himself with Jonah, who was in a great fish

> *...three days and three nights.   JONAH 1:17*

Even more significant is the Jewish custom of mourning seven days at death, but never on a sabbath. With two sabbaths in a row, Jesus precluded that we should not mourn. On the third day of his death, his family and friends could begin to mourn, but he came alive again!

Resurrection

On Sunday: On the day we now call Sunday,

> *The first day of the week cometh Mary Magdalene early, when it was yet dark, unto the sepulchre, and seeth the stone taken away from the sepulchre.*
>
> *Then she runneth, and cometh to Simon Peter, and to the other disciple...and saith unto them, They have taken away the Lord out of the sepulchre,...   JOHN 20:1-2*

Peter and the other disciple

> *...ran both together...*

And he stooping down, and looking in, saw the linen clothes lying...

> *And the napkin, that was about his head, not lying with the linen clothes, but wrapped together in a place by itself.   JOHN 20:4-7*

This location for the tomb of Jesus has a spirit about it that lifts the heart. In 1972, President Harold B. Lee said, "This is the place. He was here." Most importantly, the Garden Tomb is an empty tomb, testifying that Jesus lives.

The Talith for Burial: For Jews today, the cloth put over the head of the deceased is the talith, the garment or prayer shawl. There is a suggestion that the "napkin that was about his head" could be the Talith. The physical description of "wrapped together" seems to suggest the physical action of folding his clothes before he left the tomb.

The Tomb Was Empty: Later, Mary stood outside the sepulcher weeping; she also stooped down and looked into the sepulcher. The fact that several people are mentioned to be stooping means it must have been a small entrance.

Mary Sees Two Angels and Jesus: As the weeping Mary looked in, she saw two angels; they spoke to her; she spoke to them;

> *...she turned herself back, and saw Jesus standing, and knew not that it was Jesus.*

> *...She, supposing him to be the gardener, saith unto him, Sir, if thou have borne him hence, tell me where thou hast laid him, and I will take him away.   JOHN 20:14-15*

Jesus called her by name, and

> *...She turned herself, and saith unto him...Master.   JOHN 20:16*

He was alive again! She saw him, and Jesus spoke to her,

> *...go to my brethren, and say unto them, I ascend unto my Father, and your Father; and to my God, and your God.*

> *Mary Magdalene came and told the disciples that she had seen the Lord, and that he had spoken these things unto her.
> JOHN 20:17-18*

He Lives: That evening Jesus appeared to ten Apostles. (Thomas was not with them.) They had locked themselves in a room because of their fear of the Jewish priests. They were startled. Jesus reassuringly comforted them.

> *...and saith unto them, [Shalom, Shalom, aleichem].   JOHN 20:19*

Wounds in His Hands and Feet: He obviously spoke in their language; however, in English his expressions are just as comforting,

> *...Peace be unto you.*

> *...when he had thus spoken, he shewed them his hands and his feet...*

> *And they gave him a piece of a broiled fish, and of an honeycomb.*

> *And he took it and did eat before them.   LUKE 24:36-43*

Appearances of Jesus: Jesus appeared later to the eleven Apostles in Jerusalem and to others on the way to Emmaus. He appeared to, spoke to, and ate with several of them in Galilee.

> *And, behold, two of them went that same day to a village called Emmaus, which was from Jerusalem about threescore furlongs...*

Jesus himself drew near, and went with them...

But their eyes were holden that they should not know him...

And beginning at Moses and all the prophets, he expounded unto them in all the scriptures the things concerning himself.

And it came to pass, as he sat at meat with them, he took bread, and blessed it, and brake, and gave to them.

And their eyes were opened, and they knew him; and he vanished out of their sight.

And they said one to another, Did not our heart burn within us, while he talked with us by the way, and while he opened to us the scriptures?   LUKE 24:13-32

After these things Jesus shewed himself again to the disciples at the sea of Tiberias;...

There were together Simon Peter, and Thomas called Didymus, and Nathanael of Cana in Galilee, and the sons of Zebedee, and two other of his disciples.

Simon Peter saith unto them, I go a fishing. They say unto him, We also go with thee. They went forth, and entered into a ship immediately; and that night they caught nothing.

But when the morning was now come, Jesus stood on the shore:...

Then Jesus saith unto them, Children, have ye any meat? They answered him, No.

And he said unto them, Cast the net on the right side of the ship, and ye shall find. They cast therefore, and now they were not able to draw it for the multitude of fishes.

...Now when Simon Peter heard that it was the Lord, he girt his fisher's coat unto him...and did cast himself into the sea....

Jesus saith unto them, Come and dine...

This is now the third time that Jesus shewed himself to his disciples, after that he was risen from the dead.   JOHN 21:1-14

The New Testament has a record of over five hundred people seeing Jesus.

And when he had spoken these things, while they beheld, he was taken up; and a cloud received him out of their sight.

And while they looked steadfastly toward heaven as he went up, behold, two men stood by them in white apparel;

Which also said, Ye men of Galilee, why stand ye gazing up into heaven? this same Jesus, which is taken up from you into heaven, shall so come in like manner as ye have seen him go into heaven.
ACTS 1:9-11

After that, he was seen of above five hundred brethren at once; of whom the greater part remain unto this present...
1 CORINTHIANS 15:6

Testimonies at the Tomb: While visiting the Garden Tomb in 1972, Harold B. Lee, President of The Church of Jesus Christ of Latter-day Saints, said simply, "This is the place. He was here." This was another witness added to many in the journal of life. The Savior lives! And because he lives, so shall we. He gave us the greatest chapter in human history, the redemption of all mankind.

For almost thirty years now, I have had the privilege of bringing people to this empty tomb. My first visit was in 1973. It was an enriching experience. I cannot count the times I have returned; however, one thing is for sure: my last visit is always as sweet as the first. Most revisits have enhanced my understanding. That is because the spirit of sacred events constantly confirms the tradition of a living Messiah. The scriptural account continues to ring with truth, while the rocks and plants and creatures of life— the place—give their witness, that He lives!

The Savior's tomb is empty.

SCRIPTURAL REFERENCES (KJV)

Section Six

Epilogue

The King is Coming

 I was in Galilee with tourists on the day when the headline news called out, "The King is coming!" Children carrying flowers were sent first to cross the new bridge across the Jordan River and greet the man, Hussein, the modern-day king of Jordan. It was the year 1994. In 1951, Hussein was a child standing next to his grandfather, King Abdullah, as he was shot to death while in prayer at the Al Aksa Mosque in Jerusalem. The underlying reason for the assassination was that Grandfather Abdullah envisioned a peaceful coexistence with the Jews of Israel. Moslem fanatics apparently thought that killing the king would eliminate peace. It did not; peace was spared. Among the shots was a bullet that glanced off a medal on young Hussein's chest. His life was spared.

Somewhere tucked in the genetic code of his royal blood, Hussein was destined to become the king who would see the peace his grandfather yearned for. Although not the first peace treaty a Moslem nation would have with Israel, it is by far the warmest peace agreement Israel has with any Arab neighbor.

The joy and warmth of this peace are reflected by Arabs in Israel. I hear the question repeated almost daily, "Mister Danny, have you been to Amman yet?" I have, and I will visit again. And so will thousands of Americans, Europeans, and others of the world family. Setting aside man-made fear and going with calm hearts, they will visit the Holy Land, all of it — Israel, Egypt, and Jordan.

Jesus of Nazareth, the Holy King: The "Holy" of the land was Jesus of Nazareth. He was born in Bethlehem, moved to Egypt, returned to Galilee, visited beyond the Jordan River, and fulfilled his mission in Jerusalem, the Holy City. His influence reaches out from these places to all the world. Now, I ask you, have you been to the Holy Land? If you haven't, you should. President Spencer W. Kimball suggested that every Latter-day Saint who could afford it should visit the Holy Land. He said, "It will change your life…I went and it changed mine." The peace you will experience will warm your heart. You'll experience what the lifeblood of this land really is.

Kings in Israel: Symbolically, between the first king in this land (Saul), and the last king (Hussein), was the King of Kings. His purpose was to bring peace.

> *Peace I leave with you, my peace I give unto you: not as the world giveth, give I unto you. Let not your heart be troubled, neither let it be afraid.   JOHN 14:27*

"I welcome you soon to see, hear, and feel the gospel in its ancient environment. It will help prepare you to greet the king."

Modern peace is still preserved. The prophetic promises of peace are happening now. For awhile, Arab and Jewish children will grow up together in a new understanding of tranquility. This window of time has also opened an opportunity for you. You can be touched by the ancient culture, religion, and spirit that still reflect ancient truths that have been restored in modern times. I welcome you to soon see, hear, and feel the gospel in its ancient environment. It will help prepare you to greet the king—for soon the King of Kings will come!

Daniel Rona

Index

For information about traveling in Israel with
Daniel Rona, call 800-272-7662